Coming Home

TIMELESS WISDOM
FOR FAMILIES

JAMES C. DOBSON, PH.D.

Tyndale House Publishers, Inc.

Wheaton, Illinois

Library of Congress Cataloging-in-Publication Data

Dobson, James C., date
   Coming home : timeless wisdom for families / by James Dobson.
      p.   cm.
   ISBN 0-8423-1442-3 (alk. paper)
   1. Family—Religious life.   2. Parenting—Religious aspects—Christianity.   3. Christian life.
I. Title.
BV4526.2.D628   1998
248.4—dc21   98-45171

Printed in the United States of America

04   03   02   01   00   99   98
7   6   5   4   3   2   1

Table of Contents

Introduction

Thank you for your interest in this little book, which we have titled *Coming Home*. It is a compilation of many of my favorite commentaries addressing the subjects of children; marriage; teenagers; grandparents; blended parents; single parents; public, private, and home schools; blended families; medical research; and dozens of related topics. I hope you'll find these suggestions helpful and practical for your own home.

The concepts and ideas included in this book were drawn from a broadcast called *Focus on the Family Commentary*. It is heard daily on hundreds of radio and television stations throughout the United States and in over seventy other countries on six continents. The listening audience is estimated to be in excess of 600 million people every day.

How do we explain such broad interest in family-related topics among the peoples of the world? This appetite for information is a relatively recent development. What we are observing now, however, is that millions of husbands and wives are concerned about the enormous challenges that are plaguing the institutions of marriage and parenthood. Indeed, the human family is a small community that is facing universal problems, including divorce, drugs, infidelity, juvenile delinquency, violence, and many other difficulties. This appears to explain why families in diverse cultures are suddenly receptive to timeless advice that is based on the wisdom of the Judeo-Christian system of values.

The commentaries you are about to read were written in a ninety-second format, which makes them concise and to the point. I think you will enjoy them. Described in an earlier book of commentaries, entitled *Home with a Heart,* are words that are again applicable: "Some are practical. Some are spiritual. Some are serious. Some are humorous. And some are intended simply to inspire the 'better angels' within us. In the end, each commentary is designed to make its own small contribution to the relationships that matter most—those that thrive in the home—where the heart is."

I believe these statements will hit close to where you live. It would be a pleasure to hear from you after you have read *Coming Home.* Greetings to you and your family.

James C. Dobson, Ph.D.

In Recognition of Mothers

My commentary on this occasion is in honor of mothers around the world. There is no assignment on earth that requires the array of skills and understanding needed by a mom in fulfilling her everyday duties. She must be a resident psychologist, physician, theologian, educator, nurse, chef, taxi driver, fire marshal, and occasional police officer.

Join her on a midmorning visit to the pediatrician's office. After sitting for forty-five minutes with a cranky, feverish toddler on her lap, Mom and baby are finally ushered into the examining room. The doctor checks out the sick child and then tells the woman with a straight face, "Be sure you keep him quiet for four or five days. Don't let him scratch the rash. Make certain he keeps the medicine down, and you'll want to watch his stools."

"Yeah sure, Doc! Any other suggestions?"

"Just one. This disease is contagious. Keep your other four kids away from him. I'll see you in a week."

The amazing thing is that most mothers would get this job done—and they'd do it with love and wisdom. God made 'em good at what they do. And he gave them a passion for their children. They would, quite literally, lay down their lives to protect the kids entrusted to their care. And that's why they are deserving of our admiration—on Mother's Day, or on any other day of the year.

Keeping the Boats Together

Imagine, if you will, two little rowboats setting off to cross a choppy lake. A man sits in one, and a woman rides blissfully in the other. They have every intention of rowing side by side, but then they begin drifting in opposite directions. They can hardly hear each other above the sound of the wind. Soon the man finds himself at the northern end of the lake, and the woman bobs along at the south. Neither can recall how he or she drifted so far from the other or what they should do to reconnect.

This simple illustration has meaning for newlyweds who embark on life's journey. They stand at the altar and pledge to live together in love and harmony. Unfortunately, it doesn't always work that way. Unless their relationship is maintained and cultivated, it will grow distant and estranged. In essence, that is why romantic little rowboats often drift toward opposite ends of the lake.

The question to be raised is, How can husbands and wives remain in the same proximity for a lifetime? The answer is to row like crazy. Take time for romantic activities. Think not of yourself but of the other. Avoid that which breeds conflict and resentment. And listen carefully to the needs of the partner. These are the keys to harmony and friendship.

It's difficult to keep two rowboats floating along together, but it can be done if each partner is determine to row. Unless they are willing to paddle, however, the currents of culture will separate them forever.

The First Five Minutes

I heard about a brilliant but simple principle some years ago that I never forgot. Its thesis was based on the concept of "the first five minutes," describing the way people relate to each other. Everything they do for hours is influenced by the first moments they spend together.

For example, a speaker is given very few moments to convince his audience that he really does have something worthwhile to say. If he's boring or stilted in the beginning, his listeners will begin thinking about something else, and the orator will never understand why. If he hopes to use humor during his speech, he'd better say something funny very quickly, or his audience won't believe he can make them laugh. The opportunity of the moment is lost.

Closer to home, the first five minutes of a morning determine how a mother will interact with her children on that day. A snarl or a complaint as the kids gather for breakfast will sour their relationship for hours.

And when a man arrives home from work at the end of the day, the way he greets his wife will influence their interaction throughout the evening. If he mutters, "Not tuna casserole again!" the relationship will be put on edge from then to bedtime.

Fortunately, when we have been apart from those we love, we have an opportunity to reset the mood. A little sensitivity when coming back together can produce surprising benefits. It all depends on the first five minutes.

Chippie the Parakeet

Author Max Lucado reported a delightful story about a parakeet named Chippie, who had a very bad day. It began when the bird's owner decided to clean his cage with a vacuum cleaner. She was almost finished when the phone rang, so she turned around to answer it. Before she knew it, Chippie was gone. In a panic, she unsnapped the top of the vacuum and ripped open the bag. There was Chippie, covered in dirt and gasping for air. She carried him to the bathroom and rinsed him off under the faucet. Then realizing that Chippie was cold and wet, she reached for the hair dryer. Chippie never knew what hit him.

His owner was asked a few days later, how he was recovering.

"Well," she replied, "Chippie doesn't sing much anymore. He just sits and stares."[1]

Have you ever felt like that? One minute you're whistling through life, and the next you're caught up in a whirlwind of stress. You're running frantically through the airport and arrive at the gate just in time to see your plane take off. The table is set for guests when we see smoke curling out of the kitchen. These annoyances of life strike when we least expect them, and they always leave us dazed and disoriented.

The next time life sucks you into its vortex, hang on and make the best of it. But unlike the experience of Chippie, don't ever let the song go out of your life.

The Hurried Child

There is a tendency for parents in Western nations to make their children grow up too quickly, rushing them through the milestones of childhood and propelling them into the pressures of adolescence. This is the conclusion of developmental psychologist Dr. David Elkind, who called this cultural phenomenon the "Hurried Child Syndrome." It occurs when parents encourage their children to behave like teenagers, such as buying makeup for preschool girls, permitting teenage dating, treating kids more like grown-ups, expecting them to make adult-level decisions, dressing them in designer clothes, and especially, exposing them to explicit sexuality in movies, television, and music videos.[2]

In years past, parents understood the need for an orderly progression through childhood. There were cultural "markers" that determined the ages at which certain behaviors were appropriate. Boys, for example, wore short pants until they were twelve or thirteen. Those markers have disappeared, or they've been moved downward. It was a big mistake.

When you treat your children as if they're grown, it becomes very difficult to set limits on their adolescent behavior down the road. How can you establish a curfew for a thirteen-year-old, for example, who has been taught to think of himself or herself as an adult?

In short, the "Hurried Child Syndrome" robs our kids of childhood and places them on an unnatural timetable that's harmful to mental and physical health. Let's let our kids be kids.

Return to Mayberry

When it comes to family-related matters, I'm known as a traditionalist. In fact, there are some who think I would like to take the American family back to the days of Ozzie and Harriet. But that criticism is preposterous.

I don't want to go back to Ozzie and Harriet. I want to go back to Mayberry—with Sheriff Andy Taylor and the gang. I loved it when Barney Fife said, "My whole body's a weapon!"

Obviously, I know that Mayberry never existed—that Aunt Bea and Opie were figments of the writers' imagination. But there is validity to the theme of that sitcom. I was in high school during the "happy days" of the 1950s, and I can tell you that it was much easier to grow up in that era. I attended a racially mixed high school, yet there were no gangs there, very little alcohol, and absolutely *no* drugs. None! Most of us studied hard enough to get by, and we rather liked our parents. As for sex, there was far more talk about it than action. About once a year a girl came up pregnant; but she was packed off somewhere, and I never knew where she went. By almost any measure, kids simply fared better in those days.

Nevertheless, that era is gone forever. You can't back up on a freeway. But considering the enormous pressures on today's generation, we could make the world safer and more secure for them. And the way to start is by building stronger and more harmonious families in which they can grow.

Happily Ever After

Have you ever stopped to consider just how effectively children's traditional literature teaches kids, and especially little girls, that they must be beautiful—or else? Many of the age-old stories center around physical attractiveness in one form or another.

Take, for example, "The Ugly Duckling." This is a story about an unhappy little bird who was rejected by the better-looking ducks. Fortunately for him, he had a beautiful swan inside that surfaced in young adulthood. The story does not mention the ugly duckling who grew up to be an ugly duck!

Then there's Sleeping Beauty. Why wasn't she called Sleeping Ugly? Because the prince wouldn't have awakened her with a gentle kiss! He would have let a homely little princess go on resting.

How about Rudolph the Red-Nosed Reindeer? Rudolph had a weird nose that caused his little reindeer friends to laugh and call him names. They wouldn't let poor Rudolph join in the reindeer games. This story has nothing to do with reindeer. It has everything to do with children. This is how they treat the physically peculiar.

Don't forget Snow White, who was resented by the evil queen. That's why she asked the question, "Mirror, mirror on the wall, who's the fairest of them all?" The queen was green with envy over Snow White's stunning beauty.

And how about Dumbo the elephant? Dumbo was ridiculed for having big floppy ears until he used them to fly.

Then there is the all-time favorite: Cinderella. It wasn't the carriage and the horses that shook up the prince when she arrived at the ball. You can bet Cinderella was a pretty little thing.

These age-old stories are fun to read, and many generations of children have loved them. But we should understand their hidden messages, even if we continue to share them. There's a very serious side to the emphasis on beauty in the literature of the young. Little girls, especially, can begin to believe that those who are unattractive are unworthy as human beings. That is a very destructive idea.

Tim and Christine Burke

Would you be willing to give up your career, your aspirations, and a $600,000 annual salary if your family was in need? I know a man who did.

In 1985 Tim Burke saw his boyhood dream come true the day he was signed to pitch for the Montreal Expos. After four years in the minors, he was finally given a chance to play in the big leagues. And he quickly proved to be worth his salt—setting a record for the most relief appearances by a rookie player.

Along the way, however, Tim and his wife, Christine, adopted four children with very special needs—two daughters from South Korea, a handicapped son from Guatemala, and another son from Vietnam. All of the children were born with very serious illnesses or defects. Neither Tim nor Christine was prepared for the tremendous demands such a family would bring. And with the grueling schedule of major-league baseball, Tim was seldom around to help. So in 1993, only three months after signing a $600,000 contract with the Cincinnati Reds, he decided to retire.

When pressed by reporters to explain this unbelievable decision, he simply said, "Baseball is going to do just fine without me. But I'm the only father my children have."

Heroes are in short supply these days. Tim and Christine Burke are two of them.

A Forgotten Monument

L ast summer I was in a picturesque little town called Garmisch in southern Germany, and I happened to notice a small monument erected in memory of the young men who died in the First World War.

It caught my attention because, as an American, I've always thought of our war dead as heroes and the enemy losses as, well, the enemy. But there on a bronze plaque were the names of boys who had actually lived in that beautiful village and who suffered, bled, and died for their country. About twenty men were listed, along with their ranks and dates of death, from 1914 to 1918. I stood reading those names and wondering what stories they concealed and what their losses meant to the loved ones waiting in that little town.

Then I walked to the other side of the monument and saw another bronze plaque listing the dead from the Second World War, 1939 to 1945. Something immediately jumped out at me. Many of the last names were the same. It was obvious that the young men who had lost their lives in that Great War had left little boys behind who grew up in time to die in the next. It also meant there were women in Garmisch who lost their husbands in World War I only to have their sons die two decades later on other battlefields.

This little journey into history emphasized for me once more that it is families that suffer most from the ravages of war.

It's Never Too Late

The world seems to worship youth and is terrified of aging. But there was a time when getting older was associated with wisdom and experience. In fact, some of the greatest accomplishments in history came very late in life.

Immanuel Kant wrote one of his best philosophical works at the age of seventy-four. Verdi penned his classic "Ave Maria" at eighty-five. Alfred, Lord Tennyson was eighty when he wrote "Crossing the Bar." Michelangelo was eighty-seven when he completed *The Pietà,* his greatest work of art. Justice Oliver Wendell Holmes set down some of his most brilliant opinions at the age of ninety. Titian painted his famous *Battle of Lepanto* at the age of ninety-eight. And Ronald Reagan was the most powerful man in the world at seventy-five.[3]

Generally speaking, older people today are healthier than ever before, and anything that squanders their talents is foolish. While we're on the subject, it irritates me that television advertisers are only interested in programming for the younger set. Isn't a tube of toothpaste sold to an eighty-year-old just as profitable as one pitched to a kid?

This notion that life should be winding down at fifty or sixty years of age is crazy. I'll bet the baby boomers agree with me. They set the world on its ear when they were kids. They're not going to limp off the stage before they absolutely must, nor should you or I.

Tetherball Terror

I want to say a few words today on behalf of all those noble people who teach our boys and girls in public and private schools. I was also a teacher many years ago, and it was one of the most rewarding things I have ever done— and one of the most challenging.

I remember the morning a kid named Norbert suddenly became ill. He lost his breakfast with no warning to his fellow students or to me. I can still recall thirty-two sixth graders racing to the far corners of the room and shouting, "Eeeeuuuuyuckk!" One of them said, "I wouldn't talk, Greg. You did it last year!"

Then there was the afternoon a twelve-year-old girl named Donna asked if I wanted to play a game of tetherball. "Sure," I said. It was a big mistake. Donna was a tetherball freak. Right there in front of every kid on the playground, she drew back and spiked the ball with all her might and drove it straight up my nose. I never even saw it coming. She had my nose vibrating like a tuning fork.

It was hard on the pride of a twenty-four-year-old would-be jock, I can tell you. But those weren't the toughest aspects about teaching. I learned that it takes tons of patience, love, skill, and dedication to do the job right.

So let me tip my hat today to those men and women who head out each morning for the classroom. The future is in their hands.

Whomever

y family and I took a ski vacation in California some years ago when our children were still young. It was a memorable time but one that had its frustrating moments. Coping with two kids who are complaining about the cold and losing gloves and scarves can get on a father's nerves.

After getting them located at the lodge, I parked the car and waited for a flatbed truck to take me back to the top of the mountain. About fifteen young skiers waited with me. Then I noticed a girl in her early twenties standing with the others. When she turned to look at me, I recognized the unmistakable appearance of mental retardation in her eyes. She was behaving strangely and repeating the word *whomever* without meaning. The other young skiers smiled and rolled their eyes.

Then I noticed that the big man standing near her was her father. He had obviously seen the reactions of the other skiers. Then he did something that moved me. He put his arms around the girl, looked down lovingly at his daughter, and said, "Yeah, babe. Whomever."

This father had obviously seen the scorn in the faces of the other skiers. The compassion in his voice and his manner seemed to be saying, "Yes, it's true. She is retarded. We can't hide that fact. She is very limited in ability. She won't sing the songs. She won't write the books. In fact, she's already out of school. We've done the best we could for her. But I want you all to know something. This is my girl, and I love her. She's the whole world to me. And I'm not ashamed to be identified with her. 'Yeah, babe. Whomever!'"[4]

The tenderness of that father flooded out from his soul and engulfed mine. I quietly apologized to the Lord for complaining about my irritations and looked forward to hugging my children at the top of the mountain.

Terrors by Night

Have you ever been awakened in the middle of the night by a boy or girl who was obviously terrified but couldn't explain why? That child may have just experienced what is known as a night terror—which is very different from a nightmare. It's important to understand the difference.

If children are awakened in the midst of a nightmare, they can usually describe the "story" and tell you what was so scary about it. Then they can be comforted and tucked in for the rest of the night. But youngsters in the midst of night terrors usually can't be brought to consciousness, even though they may sit up in bed with eyes open, screaming and shaking pitifully. It's as if they're in another world that won't even be remembered the next morning.

It appears that night terrors occur in what is known as stage-four sleep, which is deeper and further from consciousness than any other human experience. In this state, the body's mechanisms are reduced to a bare minimum to sustain life. Breathing, heart rate, metabolism, and other functions go into superslow motion. Nightmares, on the other hand, occur in stage-three sleep, which means they're closer to consciousness and are linked to events in one's waking life.

The good news is that there appear to be no physical or psychological problems associated with night terrors. You can, in fact, prevent them with a mild dose of medication. However, most physicians don't recommend doing so unless they're disturbing the parents' stage-four sleep.

Night terrors and nightmares. It's a distinction worth remembering.

The Earthquake

We discussed previously a phenomenon known as night terrors, those frightening experiences that some children have while sleeping and that are very different from nightmares.

My own daughter had such an experience when she was four years old. About midnight one night, she began screaming from her bed. When I reached her side, she was babbling excitedly about the fact that the wall was about to fall on her.

She was saying, "Daddy, it's falling, it's falling. The wall is falling!" even though she wasn't awake.

I pressed the child's hand against the wall and said, "Honey, that wall has been there a long time. It's very strong. It isn't going to fall. You are OK. Go back to sleep. Everything is all right."

I don't believe Danae ever came to consciousness. I tucked her under the covers and went back to sleep myself. Six hours later, on the morning of February 9, 1971, a powerful 6.1 earthquake rattled the city of Los Angeles and shook my wife and me out of bed. I rushed to Danae's room to get her out of the way of that wall, which was violently jumping and shaking above her bed.

Did our four-year-old have some kind of forewarning of the earthquake in the midnight hours? I don't know, but I'll tell you this: The next time she tells me the wall is going to fall, I intend to believe her!

The Most Rejected Man of His Time

He began his life with all the classic handicaps and disadvantages. His mother was a dominating woman who found it difficult to love anyone. She gave him no affection, no training, and no discipline during his early years. When he was thirteen, a school psychologist commented that he probably didn't even know the meaning of the word *love*. During adolescence, the girls would have nothing to do with him and he fought with the boys.

After failing at every pursuit, including a stint in the U.S. Marine Corps, he fled the country. He married a Russian girl, but she also began to hold him in contempt. She could outfight him, and she learned to bully him. Finally, she forced him to leave.

After days of loneliness, he went home, fell on his knees, and literally begged her to take him back. He wept at her feet, but she laughed at him and made fun of his sexual impotency in front of a friend. Finally, he pleaded no more. No one wanted him. No one had ever wanted him. He was perhaps the most rejected man of his time.

The next day he was a strangely different man. He arose, went to the garage, and took down a rifle he had hidden there. He carried it with him to his newly acquired job at a book-storage building. And from a window on the sixth floor of that building, shortly after noon, November 22, 1963, he sent two shells crashing into the head of President John Fitzgerald Kennedy.

Lee Harvey Oswald—the rejected, unlovable failure—killed the man who, more than any other person on earth, embodied all the success, beauty, wealth, and family affection that Oswald lacked. In firing that rifle, he utilized the one skill he had learned in his entire, miserable lifetime.[5]

Kids Are like Kites

The task of letting our children go can be a tough one for parents. It was described by the late Erma Bombeck as being rather like flying a kite in this manner: Mom and Dad run down the road hoping to catch a breeze. Eventually, and with much effort, they manage to hoist the kite a few feet in the air. Just when they think it is safely under way, great danger looms. It dives toward electrical lines and twirls perilously near the trees. It is a scary moment. Then, unexpectedly, a gust of wind catches the kite and carries it upward. Mom and Dad begin feeding line as rapidly as they can.

The kite then becomes difficult to hold. Parents reach the end of their line and begin to wonder what to do next. The little craft demands more freedom. It rises higher and higher. Dad stands on tiptoe to accommodate the tug. It is now grasped tenuously between his index finger and thumb, held upward toward the sky. Then comes the moment of release. The string slips through Dad's fingers, and the kite soars majestically into God's beautiful sky.

The kite is now a mere pinpoint of color in the sky. The parents are proud of what they've done—but sad to realize that their job is finished. It was a labor of love. But where did the years go?[6]

Parenting is an exhilarating and terrifying experience and one that was ordained from the beginning. But with the ultimate release, the parents' task is finished. The kite is free, and so, for the first time in twenty years, are they.

Grandma's off Her Rocker

There was a time when uncles, aunts, brothers, and sisters were available to give parents a helping hand with child rearing. But more typically today, the extended family is spread all over the continent and might not be trusted anyway. Even grandparents are sometimes unavailable because they're just as busy as their kids. Let me share a humorous poem that describes this situation. I have no idea who wrote this little piece, but I think you'll enjoy it. It's called "Where Have All the Grandmas Gone?"

> *In the dim and distant past,*
> *When life's tempo wasn't fast,*
> *Grandma used to rock and knit,*
> *Crochet, tat and baby-sit.*
>
> *When the kids were in a jam,*
> *They could always call on "Gram."*
> *In that day of gracious living,*
> *Grandma was the gal for giving.*

BUT today she's in the gym,
Exercising to keep slim.
She's off touring with the bunch,
Or taking clients out to lunch.

Going north to ski or curl,
All her days are in a whirl.
Nothing seems to stop or block her,
Now that Grandma's off her rocker!!![7]

Well, now we know why Grandma isn't at home waiting for a call. I think it's wonderful that older people are busy and productive. But if that means they don't have time for grandkids, we're all the losers for it. Children need not only mothers and fathers who are dedicated to them but also older adults who are invested in their lives. The people most qualified to fulfill that responsibility are loving grandmas and grandpas who are passionately committed to their own flesh and blood.

Waiting for the Glue to Dry

D r. Desmond Morris, well-known researcher and author, spent many years studying the institution of marriage and the factors that contribute to long-term intimacy. A relationship that fails to survive, he said, can usually be traced to the dating days when the bond between a man and woman was inadequately cemented. And what interfered with the bond? It is likely to result from physical intimacy occurring too early in the relationship. Instead of taking the time to know each other—to talk and laugh and share lovers' secrets—the couple engages in early sexual activity. Such familiarity interferes with intimacy and weakens the marital bond ever after.[8]

It may be a stretch, but this understanding reminds me of my efforts to build model airplanes as a kid. My friends made wonderful planes out of balsa wood, but I could never get one finished. Why? Because I was too impatient to wait for the glue to dry. I just couldn't keep my hands off the pieces long enough for them to congeal.

Romantic relationships that begin with touching, kissing, fondling, and intercourse in the early dating days do damage to the bond. So if you want to enjoy an intimate friendship that will remain vibrant for a lifetime, the key is simple: Just keep your hands off one another until the glue dries.

Homework for Kids: Good or Bad?

How do you feel about homework being given during the elementary school years? Is it a good idea? And if so, how much is best?

Having written several books on discipline and being on record as an advocate of reasonable parental authority, my answer may surprise you: I believe homework for young children can be counterproductive if not handled very carefully. Little kids are asked to sit for five or more hours per day doing formal classwork. Many of them also take a tiring bus ride home. Then guess what? They're placed at a desk and told to do more assignments. For a wiry, active, fun-loving youngster, that's asking too much. Learning for them becomes an enormous bore instead of the exciting panorama that it ought to be.

Excessive homework during the early years also has the potential of interfering with family life. In our home we wanted our kids to participate in church activities, have some family time, and still be able to kick back and play after school. They needed to swing on the swings and play ball with their friends. Yet by the time their homework was done, darkness had fallen, dinnertime had arrived, baths were taken, and off they went to bed. Something just didn't feel quite right about that kind of pace.

Homework has a place in a child's education, but I think the time spent on after-school assignments in the early years should be very restricted. There are better things for the young to be doing after a long day in the classroom.

More Homework

L et me offer another word about homework assignments during the elementary school years. Though many educators and parents will disagree, I think time spent studying after school should be very limited.

In addition to the factors I mentioned, homework generates a considerable amount of stress for parents. Many kids either won't do the assignments, or they get tired and whine about them. That's when angry words begin to fly. I'm convinced that some frustrated parents lose their patience and subject their immature children to abusive situations.

When my wife, Shirley, was teaching second grade, one of her students came to school with both eyes black and swollen. The student reported that her father had beaten her because she couldn't learn her spelling words. That's illegal now, of course, but it was tragically tolerated in those days. That poor youngster will always think of herself as "stupid."

Then there are the parents who complete kids' assignments

themselves just to get them over the hump. Have you ever worked for two weeks on a fifth-grade geography project for your eleven-year-old and then learned later that you got a C- on it? That's the ultimate humiliation.

In short, I believe homework in elementary school is appropriate for learning multiplication tables, spelling words, and test review. It's also helpful in training kids to bring home books, remember assignments, and complete them as required. But to burden them night after night with monotonous book work is to invite educational burnout. It is unwise to do that to an immature child!

The Millionaire

I n the 1950s there was a popular television program called *The Millionaire* that featured a rich man who gave a million dollars anonymously each week to some unsuspecting person. Then we saw how the money changed the life of that individual. The outcome was always bad. Rather than solving problems or making life easier, the unexpected wealth just brought greed, violence, and conflict.

Well, that was just fiction—or was it? The truth is that sudden wealth often has precisely that effect on those who achieve it. With the spread of state lotteries throughout the United States, there are numerous new millionaires each year. We're seeing now what happens to those "lucky" people who hold the winning tickets.

Would you believe that one-third of all lottery winners go from rags to riches—to bankruptcy? And another 25 percent wind up selling the remaining payments at a discounted rate to pay off debts. A company that buys those future payments already holds $500 million in face-value jackpots. The CEO, Richard Salvato, said, "The trouble with getting all that money is that it amplifies the person's weaknesses. If they were reckless with their ordinary paychecks, they're also reckless with the bigger ones. People just don't change."[9]

So if you're fantasizing about winning the lottery and living on easy street for the rest of your life, it's probably a pipe dream. First, your chances of hitting the jackpot are infinitesimal, and second, even if you do—your troubles are just beginning. I learned that from *The Millionaire* in 1955.

How Much Is Enough?

We were talking earlier about lottery winners and what happens to those who become sudden millionaires. Follow-up studies confirm that one-third of the sudden millionaires are bankrupt within a few years. Some lose their fortunes in bad business deals, extravagant living, crazy schemes, and fast-talking relatives. They simply lack the ability to handle money—especially huge amounts of it.

But there is another great threat to unearned riches. It is likely that many of the big winners continue to gamble as before, only this time with much bigger stakes. Having won against impossible odds only convinces them that they are charmed in some way. After all, lady luck was generous last time—why not again? It would be fascinating to know how commonly multimillion-dollar purses are quickly squandered in subsequent gambling pursuits. Unfortunately, few are willing to admit it.

There's an important principle here for all of us—not just those who win jackpots. Unless you spend less than you earn, no amount of income will be enough. That's why some people get salary increases and then slide even deeper into debt. Let me say it again: *No amount of income* will be sufficient if spending is not brought under control. The *only* way to get ahead financially is to deny ourselves some of the things we want. If we don't have the discipline to do that, we will always be in debt.

Consider the finances of the United States government. It extracts more than a trillion dollars annually from American taxpayers. That's a thousand billion bucks! But in recent years our Congress outspent that enormous income by $5.6 trillion, increasing the debt by a billion dollars every thirty-two hours.[10]

The point is inescapable: Whether it be within a government or by a private individual, we have to be willing to live within our means. If we won't do that, then not even a fifteen-million-dollar jackpot will save us.

Easy come, easy go, as they say.

Rich Kids

Demographers and attorneys tell us that something dramatic is about to happen to the baby-boomer generation, which is now approaching fifty years of age. They will soon inherit more than $10.4 trillion as their parents pass from the scene. It will be the greatest transfer of wealth in the history of the world.[11] The question is, how will they handle this sudden affluence?

There may be a clue in a sociological study reported in a book by John Sedgwick called *Rich Kids*. The author made an extensive investigation of those who inherit large trust funds. He concluded that sudden wealth can be dangerous. For some, not having to work can lead to irresponsible living and addictive behavior, such as gambling and alcoholism. Money can also tear marriages to threads. Finally, absolutely nothing will divide siblings quicker than money, setting up fights over family businesses and resentment of those designated to run them.[12]

There are exceptions to these negative consequences, of course.

Some people handle wealth and power gracefully. But it is a risky passage at best and one that requires a great deal of maturity and self-control. At the least, wealthy parents should ask themselves some important questions, especially if their heirs are young. Should they remove the very challenges that helped Mom and Dad succeed in the early days—the obligation to work hard, live frugally, save, build, and produce by the sweat of their brows? And even if their sons and daughters *are* able to handle a generous inheritance, how will their grandchildren and future generations respond?

I know my views on this subject are unconventional. One of the reasons people work hard is so their children and future heirs won't have to. They love their kids and want to make things easier for them. Even so, giving a large trust fund to those who don't earn it should be done only with the greatest care and preparation.

It takes a steady hand to hold a full cup!

Dad, I Never Really Knew You

Several months ago I talked to a man who described one of the most painful experiences of his life. When he was seventeen years old, he was one of the stars on his high school football team. But his father, a very successful man in the city, was always too busy to come see him play.

Quickly the final game of the season came around, which happened to have been the state championship. The boy was desperate to have his dad there. The night of the big game, he was on the field warming up when he looked into the stadium just in time to see his father arrive with two other men, each wearing a business suit. They stood talking together for a moment or two and then left.

The man who told me this story is now fifty-eight years of age, and yet he had tears streaming down his cheeks as he relived that moment so long ago. It's been forty years since that night, and yet the rejection and pain are as vivid as ever. I was struck again by the awesome influence a father has in the lives of his children. When he is uninvolved, when he doesn't love or care for them, it creates a vacuum that reverberates for decades.

My friend's father died not long ago, and as he stood by his dad's body in the mortuary, he said, "Dad, I never really knew you. We could have shared so much love together—but you never had time for me."

Preventing Deafness

I want to offer a word of caution today about excessive noise—especially that which bombards the ears of our kids. Otologists tell us that because our hearing apparatus is a mechanical instrument that is subject to wear, overuse is often related to deafness in old age.

This fact was demonstrated by a study of natives living in a quiet village in an isolated Amazon rain forest. They rarely heard noises louder than a squawking parrot or the sounds of children laughing and playing. Not surprisingly, their hearing remained almost perfect into old age. There was virtually no deafness known to the tribe.

By contrast, living in a noisy environment continually operates the three delicate bones in the middle ear and decreases hearing acuity. Motorcycles, garbage trucks, television, and high-powered machines all take their toll. But children and young people are particularly at risk because of their music. You can imagine the effect of a Walkman or other stereo equipment blasting away at their ears for a decade or more.

Attending a Rolling Stones concert is equivalent to being strapped to the bottom of a jet airplane that is taking off or to being tied to the hood of a Mack truck going sixty miles an hour. Pete Townshend, lead singer of the legendary rock group The Who, is almost totally deaf in one ear from standing near powerful sound equipment.[13]

Quite obviously, parents should try to protect the hearing of their children. That's a tough assignment in today's youth culture, but it's worth the effort.

That's OK, Jake

Dick Korthals, one of our volunteers here at Focus on the Family, described his experience while attending a dog show. As part of the competition, a dozen dogs were commanded to "Stay!" and then expected to remain statuelike for eight minutes, while their owners left the ring. Judges scored them on how well they were able to hold their composure during their master's absence.

About four minutes into the exercise, Dick noticed a magnificent German shepherd named Jake sitting at the end of the line. It became apparent immediately that he was losing his poise, slinking slowly toward the ground. By the time his trainer returned, poor Jake was lying flat on his stomach with his head on his paws.

Jake saw the disappointment in his owner's eyes and began crawling toward him on his belly. Everyone was expecting the trainer to scold the dog for his poor performance. Instead, he bent down, cupped the dog's head in his hands, and said with a smile, "That's OK, Jake. We'll do better next time." It was a very touching moment.[14]

There's a lesson here for every parent, too. It's inevitable that our children will disappoint us. Our natural reaction when they fail is to bark at them, saying, "Why didn't you do it right?!" and, "How could you have been so stupid?!" But if we're wise, we'll remember their immaturity and imperfection.

That is the moment to say with a hug, "That's OK, my child. We'll do better next time."

MacArthur

The year was 1962, and General Douglas MacArthur was by then an old and feeble man. He had been one of the greatest military heroes of all time, leading our armies in World Wars I and II and in Korea. By then his better days were behind.

MacArthur had returned that day to his beloved West Point, where he had been a cadet some sixty years before. He had come that day to say good-bye. His speech on the Plain that day was one of the most powerful ever given. It was entitled "Duty, Honor, Country" and ended with these words:

> The shadows are lengthening for me. The twilight is here. My days of old have vanished—tone and tints. They have gone glimmering through the dreams of things that were. Their memory is of wondrous beauty, watered by tears and coaxed and caressed by the smiles of yesterday. I listen, then, but with thirsty ear, for the

witching melody of faint bugles blowing reveille, of far drums beating the long roll.

In my dreams I hear again the crash of guns, the rattle of musketry, the strange mournful mutter of the battlefield. But in the evening of my memory, I come back to West Point. Always there echoes and re-echoes, 'Duty, Honor, Country.' Today marks my final roll call with you, but I want you to know that when I cross the river, my last conscious thoughts will be of the Corps, and the Corps, and the Corps. I bid you farewell.[15]

General Douglas MacArthur died less than two years later on April 5, 1964. It seems fitting that we who enjoy the sweet benefits of freedom pause to thank the general and millions of others in uniform who died in the defense of liberty. We owe them an enormous debt. They lived by a code of "Duty, Honor, Country!"

A Simple Bag of Groceries

few years ago I slipped into a market to buy a few groceries for lunch. Standing in front of me at the checkout was an elderly woman who didn't seem to be altogether lucid. It quickly became obvious that she had selected more food than she could pay for, as she fumbled in her purse frantically for a few more coins. The checker politely continued to add up the items.

"I just don't understand where my money is," said the old lady as she made another desperate foray into the depths of her purse.

With that, I whispered to the checker, "Just go ahead and total her bill, then accept whatever money she has and put the rest on my bill."

That's what she did, and I paid an extra eight dollars to make up the difference. The old woman never knew that I had helped her. She shuffled off with her cart, relieved that her groceries had cost exactly the amount of money she was able to locate. Then I looked back at the checker and saw that she was crying. I asked her why.

"Because," she said, "I've been doing this work for twenty years, and I've never seen anyone do something like that before."

It was no big deal—an insignificant eight dollars—but simple kindness is so unusual today that it shocks us when it occurs. I'll tell you this: That may have been the best eight dollars I ever spent! I only wish I'd paid the rest of the dear lady's bill.

Respect for the Elderly

Many years ago I saw a documentary television program that I never forgot. It focused on the life of an elderly woman named Elizabeth Holt Hartford, who lived alone in a Los Angeles slum. These were her parting words that were aired on videotape a few weeks after her death:

"You see me as an old lady who's all broken down with age. But what you don't understand is that this is me in here. I'm trapped in a body that no longer serves me. It hurts, and it's wrinkled and diseased. But I haven't changed. I'm still the person I used to be when this body was young."

Those who are younger may find it difficult to appreciate Mrs. Hartford's words. She was speaking of the "Unwanted Generation" and what it is like to be aged in a time dominated by the very young; to be unable to see or hear well enough; to have an active mind that is hopelessly trapped in an inactive body; to be dependent on busy children; to be virtually sexless, emotionally and physically, in an eroticized society; to be unable to produce or contribute anything really worthwhile; and to have no one who even remembers your younger days.

A gastroenterologist once told me that 80 percent of his older patients have physical symptoms caused by emotional problems. Despair is quickly translated into bodily disorders. Obviously, self-worth is essential to well-being at all ages. Let's extend our love and respect to those such as Elizabeth Holt Hartford who have passed their prime.

No More Showers

When I was a teenager, all the students were required to shower after gym class at school. The coach would look us over to make sure we were clean before sending us on our way. Students who didn't shower didn't receive a passable grade. But those days are just about over.

The heightening sensitivity of kids today makes them unwilling to disrobe in front of one another. They vary so much in maturity during the middle school years that some are grown and others are still little prepubescent kids. Thus, it is humiliating for the undeveloped youngster to put his or her body on display in front of the wolf pack.

I served as a school psychologist in earlier days and dealt with this problem. I remember a high school sophomore who absolutely refused to shower because of the ridicule he was getting. After seeing what was happening, I agreed that he shouldn't be forced to humiliate himself in front of his friends five days a week. I successfully pled his case to the coach.

That lad's reaction was unusual twenty years ago. Today it is common. The body consciousness of our culture has sensitized many children and teenagers to their imperfections. Thus, school showers are being phased out. Another reason is that coaches and teachers have become leery of false charges of sexual abuse.[16]

The outcome? Teachers have to work in classrooms populated by adolescents who smell like gymnasiums—or worse. It's a sign of the times.

Lowering Expectations

Astrophysicist Stephen Hawking may be the most intelligent man on earth, being compared by some to Albert Einstein. But Hawking has a rare degenerative neuromuscular disorder called amyotraphic lateral sclerosis (ALS syndrome). It has left him virtually paralyzed. He manipulates a computer with the tips of his fingers and thereby communicates his calculations and thoughts.

Dr. Hawking has offered a very insightful perspective on his disorder. He said that before becoming ill he was bored by what he called "a pointless existence." He drank too much and did very little work. But after learning that he had only two years to live, life suddenly took on new meaning. He was actually happier than before.

Hawking explained the paradox this way: "When one's expectations are reduced to zero, one really appreciates everything that one does have."[17]

It's true. Everything becomes meaningful to those who are dying: a sunrise, a walk in the park, the laughter of children. But those who believe life owes them a free ride are often miserable. The high incidence of depression in Western nations, and maybe even the tragic rate of divorce, are linked in part to unrealistic expectations.

May I suggest that we accept our circumstances as they are and not demand more than life can deliver?

I Wish . . .

A sixth-grade teacher shared with me the results of a creative-writing project assigned to her class. She asked the kids to complete a series of sentences that began with the phrase "I wish . . ." The teacher expected her students to write about bicycles, toys, animals, and trips to theme parks. She was wrong. Instead, twenty of the thirty students made references to the breakup of their families or conflict at home. These are some of their actual comments:

"I wish my parents wouldn't fight, and I wish my father would come back."

"I wish I would get straight A's so my dad would love me."

"I wish my mother didn't have a boyfriend."

"I wish I had one mom and one dad so the kids wouldn't make fun of me. I have three moms and three dads, and they botch up my life."

"I wish I had an M-1 rifle so I could shoot those who make fun of me."

I know it's hardly front-page news that the family is in trouble today, but it continues to distress me to see little children like these struggling at a time when simply growing up is a major undertaking. Millions of their peers are caught in the same snare. Every aspect of their young lives is influenced by family instability during their developmental years. Without gaining access to professional counseling somewhere along the way, many of these kids will drag their problems into future relationships. Then the pattern of disintegration will repeat itself in the next generation.

Returning to the responses given to the sixth-grade students, I wonder how your *own* children would complete a sentence that began with the words "I wish . . ." You might want to ask them sometime.

Differing Assumptions

One of the most common sources of conflict between husbands and wives comes down to a simple matter of differing assumptions. Let me illustrate.

Some years ago I went through a very hectic period of my life professionally. I was a full-time professor in a medical school, but I was also traveling and speaking far more often than usual. I completely exhausted myself during that time. It was a dumb thing to do, but I had made commitments that I simply had to keep.

Finally on a concluding Friday night the siege was over, and I came dragging home. I had earned a day off, and I planned to kick back and watch a USC-Alabama football game that Saturday. Shirley, on the other hand, also felt that she had paid her dues. For six weeks she had taken care of the kids and run the home. It was entirely reasonable that I spend my Saturday doing things she wanted done around the house. Neither of us was really wrong. Both had a right to feel as we did. But the two ideas were incompatible.

Those assumptions collided about ten o'clock Saturday morning when Shirley asked me to clean the backyard umbrella. I had no intention of doing it. There was an exchange of harsh words that froze our relationship for three days.

It's important to understand that neither of us was looking for a fight, yet we both felt misunderstood and wounded by the other. Our conflict was typical of what goes on every day in a million other homes. It all comes down not to deliberate antagonism but to something called "differing assumptions."

We can avoid most of these clashes simply by making sure that the two people know what is on the other's mind. They might still disagree, but the unpleasant surprises can be prevented.

Dear Friends and Gentle Hearts

O n an icy January morning many years ago, a man was found naked and bleeding in a twenty-five-cent-a-night flophouse. Doctors sewed up the gash in his throat as best they could, but the wound and the booze had taken their toll. That night he died in his sleep.

A nurse gathering his belongings found a dirty coat with only thirty-eight cents in one pocket and a scrap of paper in the other, on which five words were written: "Dear friends and gentle hearts." *Almost like the words of a song,* she thought. And she was right. This old man turned out to have been the songwriter who penned some of America's most beloved music, including "Swanee River," "Oh! Susanna!" "My Old Kentucky Home," and hundreds more. He was Stephen Foster.[18]

That true story comes to mind whenever I see a derelict—a down-and-outer—on the street today. That dirty, sotted man or woman wasn't always in that condition. He or she was once a little baby, bubbling with promise and hope—before being cut down by the pruning knife of time. A wrong choice or two—an unfortunate circumstance at a critical moment—led to the tragedy of a wasted life.

It's difficult to see beyond a bleary-eyed bum sleeping on a park bench today, but there is a person of value within that exterior. He or she might be another creative genius at the end of a long and bitter journey.

The Apology

Have you ever found the courage to say "I'm sorry" to a child? It is difficult to do, and my father was never very good at it. I remember working with him in the backyard when I was fifteen years of age, on a day when he was particularly irritable for some reason. He crabbed at me for everything I did, even though I tried to please him. Finally, he yelled at me for something petty, and I had had enough. I threw down the rake and quit. Defiantly, I walked across our property and down the street as my dad demanded that I come back. It was one of the few occasions I ever took him on like that!

I meandered around town for a while, wondering what would happen to me when I finally went home. I ended up at my cousin's house on the other side of town. After several hours there, I admitted what I had done, and my uncle urged me to phone. With knees quaking, I called my dad.

"Stay there," he said. "I'm coming over."

To say that I was scared would be an understatement. Dad arrived in a short time and asked to see me alone.

"Bo," he began. "I didn't treat you right this afternoon. I was riding your back for no good reason, and I'm sorry. Your mom and I want you to come home now."

It was a tough moment for him, but he made a friend for life. And in so doing, he taught me something about apologizing that would someday be useful to me as a father.

Rumspringa

The task of letting go of our grown children after adolescence is one of the most difficult assignments in the entire realm of parenting. The duel dangers, of course, are doing it either too early or too late. Let me tell you how the Amish turn loose their children.

They keep their children under very tight control when they are young. Strict discipline and harsh standards of behavior are imposed from infancy. But when children turn sixteen years of age, they enter a period called "Rumspringa." Suddenly, all restrictions are lifted. They are free to drink, smoke, or behave in ways that horrify their parents. Some do just that. Most don't. They're even granted the right to leave the Amish community if they choose. But if they stay, it must be in accordance with the social order. The majority accept the heritage of their families, not because they must, but because they choose to.

Although I admire the Amish and many of their approaches to child rearing, I believe the Rumspringa concept is implemented too precipitously for children raised in a more open society. I've seen families grant "instant adulthood" to their adolescents, to their families' regret.

Instead, I recommend that parents begin transferring tiny elements of independence literally in toddlerhood. Each year more responsibility and freedom must be given to the child so that the final release in early adulthood is merely a small step rather than a leap off a cliff.

Loving Hands

Human hands. They perform marvelous functions, from those of a concert pianist to those of a brain surgeon. With the thumb in apposition to the fingers to facilitate grasping, and with the concentration of sensory nerves in the pads for evaluating the texture and the temperature of our world, human hands are a marvel of design. But they are much more than precision machinery. They carry great meaning because of what they represent to us eventually.

My mother had soft, feminine hands, and she used them when I was small to stroke my hair and rub my back. Her touch conveyed love to me in a way that compared with nothing else. I remember visiting her in a nursing home shortly before her death and looking again at those familiar hands. They were wrinkled and palsied by that time, yet they were still beautiful to me. How hard she worked to make life easy for me.

What I remember most about my father was the size of his hands. They engulfed mine and made me proud and secure as I trotted along beside him on the street. He used those hands to teach me how to cast with a rod and reel, how to draw and paint. I had seen him hold a King James Bible at least ten thousand times, thoughtfully turning the pages as he studied the Scripture. Soon those beloved hands would be folded across his chest in stillness.

The pressing question for parents is how your children will remember your hands. Hopefully, they will convey warmth, security, and protection. They should provide comfort and affirmation—but never abuse or neglect. If you do your job properly, then your hands, like those of my parents, will leave a lasting legacy of love.

No Place to Hide

ave you ever fantasized about running away from all the pressures and stresses of today's high-tech world? Surely there is a place somewhere on the globe where the pace is slower and the living is easy. Why don't we just pack up and transplant ourselves there—lock, stock, and family dog?

That dream motivated a family in 1940 to move to an island called Guadalcanal in the Coral Sea. But two years later war broke out in the Pacific, and the couple found themselves witnessing a battle in their front yard. Obviously, they had chosen the wrong place.

Where can today's families go to escape the noise and hubbub of city life? How about a small island in the Caribbean south of Cuba, called Grand Cayman? Vacationers to this resort say it is the closest thing to paradise on earth. The six thousand residents pay no taxes.[19] The water around them is calm and warm, and there are orchids growing every-where. Sounds good, doesn't it? But there's a catch. Recent medical studies revealed that the two major ailments suffered by the citizens of Grand Cayman are "hypertension" and "anxiety neuroses." Life on a tropical beach is not what it appears.

Could it be that the stresses and pressures with which we struggle actually come from within? They will plague us no matter where we live until we learn to deal with circumstances as they are. We might as well stay and bloom where we're planted, because there's simply no place to hide.

Jeep Fenders

Children can be hateful to each other, especially when adults haven't taught them basic kindness and sensitivity. I learned that when I was only eight years old.

I regularly attended a Sunday school in those days, and a visitor entered the class one morning and sat down. He said his name was Fred. I can still see his face. More important, I can still see Fred's ears. They were curved in the shape of a *C* and protruded noticeably. For some reason they reminded me of jeep fenders. Without thinking of Fred's feelings, I pointed out this strange characteristic to my friends, who all thought "Jeep Fenders" was a terribly funny name for a boy with bent ears. Fred seemed to think it was funny, too, and he chuckled along with the rest of us.

Suddenly, Fred stopped laughing. He jumped to his feet, red in the face (and ears), and rushed to the door, crying. He bolted into the hall and ran from the building. Fred never returned to our class. I remember my shock over Fred's violent and unexpected reaction. I had no idea that I was embarrassing him by my little joke. Looking back on the episode, however, I believe that my teachers and parents were largely responsible for that event. They should have told me what it feels like to be laughed at, especially when it concerns something different about our bodies.

Children can be taught to be sensitive to the feelings of others. But in the absence of that teaching, they can be brutal to one another. Another "Jeep Fenders" is out there somewhere today. Protect him or her from ridicule!

The Bulldog and the Scottie

When I was about ten years old, I loved a couple of dogs that belonged to two families in our neighborhood. One was a black Scottie, who liked to retrieve tennis balls, and the other was a pug bulldog, who had a notoriously bad temper.

One day as I was tossing the ball for the Scottie, I decided to throw it in the direction of the grouch. It was an awful mistake. The bulldog grabbed the Scottie by the throat and wouldn't let go. Neighbors came running as the Scottie screamed in pain. It took ten minutes and a garden hose to pry loose the bulldog's grip, and by then the Scottie was almost dead. He spent two weeks in the vet hospital, and I spent two weeks in the "doghouse." I regret throwing that ball to this day.

I've thought about that experience many times and its application to human relationships. Indeed, it is a simple thing to precipitate a fight. All that's necessary is to toss a ball, symbolically, under the more aggressive of the two. This is done by revealing negative comments made by one or by baiting the first in the presence of the other. It can also be accomplished very easily in business by assigning overlapping territory to two managers.

Again, the leader can start a terrible fight by tossing a ball in the right (or wrong) direction. The natural jealousy and antagonism of competitors will do the rest.

Fresh Graves

I've recently become aware of an outrageous and tragic situation occurring in Brazil and other Latin American countries. It concerns the plight of unwanted street children who are suffering unthinkable abuse.

It's been estimated that in Brazil alone, between 6 and 10 million kids live on the streets with no adult supervision. They have no families and no means of support, so they form lawless packs, begging and stealing for food during the day, then huddling together for warmth at night. Prostitution, crime, and disease are their way of life. Some of them actually live in sewers like rats. Roughly two-thirds of the young girls either commit suicide or are murdered before their eighteenth birthday.[20]

The police look on these children as vermin to be exterminated. Unbelievably, they shoot them to clean up the city. A recent news story revealed that approximately three children per day are hunted down and killed on the streets of Rio de Janeiro. A few years ago when the Earth Summit was held in that city, large numbers of homeless children were rounded up and murdered before the dignitaries arrived.[21] CNN televised row upon row of fresh little graves, where the children were buried.

I wonder sometimes if the world is any more civilized now than it was sixty years ago when the Nazis began gassing their victims. It's time for us to speak out against this brutality and to support humanitarian organizations that can help.

How can we do less?

Babies Are Listening

Be careful what you say in the presence of your babies. That's the advice of a researcher at Johns Hopkins University, who tells us that children only eight months of age are capable of hearing and remembering words, good or bad.

"Little ears are listening," says Dr. Peter Juscyzk. Babies in this study, which appears in the prestigious journal *Science,* were exposed to three recorded stories for a period of about ten days. Two weeks later they were tested in the lab and clearly recognized the words in the stories, while failing to respond to those they hadn't heard. Robin Chapman, a language specialist at the University of Wisconsin, emphasized the importance of this study. It demonstrates that very young children do attend to the sounds of language and are able to pick out those that are familiar.

"These findings are significant to parents because they tell us that reading to children at an early age can be beneficial to language development, even if they don't appear to comprehend. Reading also starts the process of learning how words are formed and used. It helps babies segment sounds out of speech," said Dr. Juscyzk.[22]

Finally, the study shows, according to Chapman, that "a lot of language learning is happening in the first year of life. It shows that parents should talk to their children and that children will learn about language from that talk."[23]

Interesting stuff—but mothers have known it intuitively for five thousand years!

Children at Risk

From 1985 to 1986 I served on the U.S. Attorney General's Commission on Pornography, which turned out to be one of the most difficult assignments of my life. For eighteen months I had the unenviable responsibility, with ten other commissioners, of examining the most wretched material ever published. Many people think obscenity consists of airbrushed nudity as seen in popular men's magazines. In reality, much of it involves graphic violence against women, depictions of bestiality, the killing of children, and other subjects that I can't describe in this setting. Our commission ultimately made twenty-six recommendations for changes in the law, each of which was passed by Congress and signed by the president.[24]

I regret to say, unfortunately, that the progress we made in the fight against obscenity has been lost. There are no limits now because of the Internet. Everything we witnessed during that investigation can be accessed by any twelve-year-old child with a computer and a modem. He or she can log on to Web sites that are clearly illegal. Material can be printed on high-resolution copiers that equal anything found in adult stores.

Not only can these images be found on the Internet—they can't be avoided. Kids are lured with attractive bait designed to snare the innocent. For example, clicking on "toys" can introduce them to sex toys; clicking on "love horses" can produce images of bestiality; clicking on "little girls" can introduce child pornography or those who prey on kids.

As a child psychologist, I want to emphasize that obscenity is *terribly* destructive to boys and girls. It is especially dangerous to boys in the early adolescent years. It can lead to lifelong addictions and teach them to associate sex with violence.

Despite these dangers, our United States Supreme Court has ruled that the law designed to protect children from this curse is unconstitutional.[25] What a shame!

Let me plead with parents to monitor what your kids are doing on that innocent-looking computer. To put a desktop or a laptop in a child's bedroom is tantamount to inviting a stranger into your home and giving him or her access to your most precious possession!

Myelinization

Have you ever wondered why an infant is unable to reach for an object or attempt to control the movement of his hands or feet? It's because the nervous system is inadequately insulated at birth. Electrical impulses are lost on their journey from the brain to other parts of the body. As the child grows, a whitish substance called myelin begins to coat the nerve fibers, allowing controlled muscular action to occur.

Myelinization typically proceeds from the head downward and from the center of the body outward. This is why a child can control the movement of his head and neck before the rest of the body, and the shoulder before the elbow, wrist, and fingers.

This understanding of myelin is important to the parents of boys, especially, who are slower to develop. Because a child's visual apparatus is among the last mechanism to be insulated, some immature boys and girls are unable to read, write, or spell until later. This helps explain why late bloomers often have early learning problems in school.

Unfortunately, our culture permits few exceptions or deviations from the established educational timetable. Most six-year-olds start first grade whether they are ready or not. Some are not ready! Immature children should be home schooled or held out for a year. Most important, parents should be careful not to demand achievement from a child who is slow to develop. It may be physiologically impossible for him or her to match the successes of peers for a time, and that can be harmful.

Give myelinization a chance to do its work before challenging an undeveloped nervous system!

Echo from Eternity

Vince Foster served as deputy counsel to U.S. president Bill Clinton until the night of July 20, 1993, when he allegedly committed suicide in a Washington, D.C., park.[26] Controversy has swirled around the circumstances of his death to this day.

Regardless of where you come down on that issue, I want to share something related to it that I think you'll find interesting. Just eight weeks before his death, Foster was asked to speak to students graduating from the University of Arkansas School of Law. This is what he told the students on that occasion:

> A word about family. You have amply demonstrated that you are achievers willing to work hard, long hours and set aside your personal lives. But it reminds me of that observation that no one was ever heard to say on a deathbed: I wish I had spent more time at the office. Balance wisely your professional life and your family

life. If you are fortunate to have children, your parents will warn you that your children will grow up and be gone before you know it. I can testify that it is true. God only allows us so many opportunities with our children to read a story, go fishing, play catch, and say our prayers together. Try not to miss a one of them.[27]

Vince Foster's words now echo back to us from eternity. To paraphrase his message: While you're climbing the ladder of success, don't forget your own family.

The Walleyed Pike

L et me tell you something interesting about the walleyed pike, which is a large fish with a prodigious appetite for minnows. Something surprising happens when a plate of glass is slipped into a tank of water, placing the pike on one side and the minnows on the other. The pike can't see the glass and solidly hits the barrier in pursuit of its dinner. Again and again it swims into the glass and bumps whatever one calls the front end of a walleye.

Eventually, the pike gives up. The fish apparently concludes that the minnows are not available. It will no longer try to catch them. At that point, the glass can be removed from the tank, allowing the minnows to swim around their mortal enemy in perfect safety. The pike will not molest them. It knows what it knows: They are unreachable. Amazingly, the walleyed pike will actually starve to death while surrounded by abundant amounts of food.[28]

This illustration is relevant not only to fish but in a interesting way to children. Just as a walleyed pike can become discouraged when faced with persistent failure, boys and girls react to it similarly. Early embarrassment or frustration in the classroom, such as an inability to read or spell, can have serious implications for kids. By the second or third year, some give up on school. Success is simply not available for them.

It is critical to obtain tutorial assistance for immature little kids who get off to a bad start. Early educational intervention may help them avoid giving up on "minnows" before it is too late.

Togetherness

L et me ask you to take in a deep breath of air and hold it for a moment. Then exhale it.

You might be interested to know that this single breath of air contains at least three nitrogen atoms that were inhaled by every person who has ever lived, including Leonardo da Vinci, Winston Churchill, and Abraham Lincoln. Likewise, each of the dinosaurs in their time breathed some of the same nitrogen atoms that you took into your body. And the air that you just exhaled will circle the globe in the next twelve months and will be breathed by at least one or two of those individual atoms.

That scientific fact dramatizes the connectedness between us as human beings. Just as we share our chemistry with other members of the human family, we are all interdependent socially. We are affected positively or negatively by the actions of each other. During the self-centered days of what used to be called the "me" generation, it was common to hear people say, "As long as I'm not hurting anyone, it's nobody's business what I do." Unfortunately, everything we do affects other people, and there's no such thing as a completely independent act.

The poet John Donne wrote: "No man is an island, entire of itself, every man is a piece of a continent, a part of the main."[29] How true were his words.

The Lollipop

A mother named Elaine told me a very moving story about her three-year-old daughter, Beth, who was the youngest child in their neighborhood. She toddled after the big kids but understood that they didn't really want her along.

One day this mother looked out her kitchen window and saw Beth standing at a fence, watching the other children playing baseball. They wouldn't let her play, of course, and it was upsetting her. Suddenly, the little girl turned and ran into the house calling, "Lollipop, Mom! I need lollipop!"

Elaine went to the cupboard and handed the child a lollipop.

"No! No! Mommy," Beth said. "I want lots of lollipops."

The mother knew something was up, so she gave the child an armload of lollipops. Beth then ran back to her place at the fence and stood there silently, holding the lollipops out to the other children. She was trying to buy their acceptance—but they didn't notice her. Finally, one of the bigger kids saw Beth and yelled to the others. They ran over and grabbed the treats away from the toddler and then went back to play without even thanking her. Elaine stood watching at the window with a lump in her throat. The gifts were gone—and so were Beth's friends.

How many insecure teenagers give everything they have—including their own bodies—to gain acceptance from their peers? Then they are left standing at the fence, alone and rejected—with their lollipops gone. These are among the most painful experiences of a lifetime—for adolescents *and* for their parents. There are times when moms and dads can do nothing to help their children except to stand at the window, praying that God will get them through it!

Nature or Nurture?

For many decades behavioral scientists believed that newborns arrived into the world completely devoid of personality. The environment then stamped its unique characteristics on boys and girls during their developmental years. At one time most of the best-known psychologists in the world ascribed to this theory. Unfortunately, they were wrong.

We know now that heredity plays the larger role in the development of human temperament. This is the conclusion of meticulous research conducted over many years at the University of Minnesota. The researchers identified more than one hundred identical twins who had been separated near the time of birth. They were raised in varying cultures, religions, and locations, and for a variety of reasons. Because each set of twins shared the same genetic structure, it became possible for the researchers to examine the impact of inheritance by comparing their similarities and their differences on many variables. From these and other studies, it became clear that much of the personality, perhaps 70 percent or more, is inherited. Our genes influence such qualities as creativity, wisdom, loving-kindness, vigor, longevity, intelligence, and even the joy of living.[30]

Consider the brothers known as the "Jim twins," who were separated until they were thirty-nine years old. Their similarities were astonishing. Both married women named Linda. Both had dogs named Toy. Both suffered from migraine headaches. Both chain-smoked. Both liked beer. Both drove Chevys, and both served as sheriff's deputies. Their personalities and attitudes were virtual carbon copies.[31] This has become a very familiar pattern seen by researchers.

What do these findings mean? Are we mere puppets on a string, playing out a predetermined course without free will or personal choices? Not at all. Unlike birds and mammals that act according to instinct, humans are capable of rational thought and independent action. We don't act on every sexual urge, for example, despite our genetic underpinnings. What is clear is that heredity provides a nudge in a particular direction—a definite impulse or inclination—but one that can be brought under the control of our rational processes.

Obviously, these findings are of enormous significance to our understanding of human behavior. It changes everything, especially our understanding of children.

Mom Goes to School

I want to tell you about my mother, who was a master at trench warfare during my stubborn adolescent years. I could never hide anything from her for long, and she knew, intuitively, that I was getting into trouble at school.

One day she sat me down and said firmly, "I know you have been fooling around and giving your teachers a hard time. Well, I've thought it over, and I've decided that I'm not going to do anything about it. I'm not going to punish you. I'm not going to take away privileges. I'm not even going to talk about your foolishness anymore."

I was smiling until she added, "But I do want you to understand one thing. If the principal or the teachers ever call me, I promise you that the next day I'm going to school with you. I'll walk two feet behind you all day. I'll hold your hand in front of all your friends. When you sit in class, I'll climb into the seat with you. For one full day, you won't be able to shake me off."

That threat absolutely terrified me. It would have been social suicide to have my mother following me in front of my friends. No punishment would have been worse! Beat me, but don't go to school with me! I'm sure my teachers wondered why there was such a remarkable improvement in my behavior near the end of my freshman year in high school.

You might try my mom's approach with your teenagers. But please—don't tell them where you got the idea.

Princess Diana

Diana, princess of Wales, was arguably one of the most glamorous and beautiful women in the world. Paparazzi hounded her for photographs right to the last moments of her life. During the latter years, Diana could generate more support for a particular cause or charity than any other celebrity.

Given this enormous influence—this glamour and beauty—isn't it interesting that the princess disliked what she saw in the mirror? She struggled with a poor body image that led to an eating disorder known as bulimia. How could a woman of such remarkable charm fall victim to self-loathing and depression?

Perhaps Diana's poor self-concept wasn't as strange as it might have seemed. Our value system, promoted so vigorously by Hollywood and the entertainment industry, is arranged so that very few women feel particularly good about their physical appearance. Even the Miss America or Miss Universe competitors will admit, if they're honest, that they are aware of their physical flaws. If those who are blessed with great beauty often deal with self-hatred, imagine how immature, gangly teenagers feel about the imperfect bodies with which they're born.

The beauty cult infects hundreds of millions of people with a sense of inadequacy and inferiority. Indeed, even Diana, princess of Wales, fell into its snare.

Who's at Fault?

I want to say a word or two today on behalf of the public schools, and especially to the men and women who serve our children there.

First, let me acknowledge that I share the concern of many others about falling test scores, increasing violence on campuses, and the high illiteracy rate. On the other hand, it is not fair to blame educators for all that has gone wrong. The teachers and school administrators who guide our children have been among the most maligned and underappreciated people in our society. It's a bum rap.

We would still be having serious difficulties in our schools if the professionals did everything right. Why? Because what goes on in the classroom can't be separated from the problems occurring in the culture at large. Educators aren't responsible for the condition of our kids when they arrive at school each morning. It's not the teachers' fault that families are unraveling and that large numbers of their students have been abused, neglected, and undernourished. They can't keep kids from watching mindless television or violent videos until midnight or from using illegal substances and alcohol. In essence, when the culture begins to crumble, the schools will also look bad.

Even though I disagree with some of the trends in modern education, I sympathize with the dedicated teachers and principals out there who are doing their best on behalf of our youngsters. They're a discouraged lot today, and they need our support.

The Last Leaf on the Tree

Let me share a classic poem about old age entitled, "The Last Leaf on the Tree." It is a favorite of mine written by Oliver Wendell Holmes.

I saw him once before as he passed by the door and again.
The pavement stones resound as he toddles o'er the ground with his cane.

They say that in his prime, e'er the pruning knife of time cut him down,
not a better man was found by the crier on his round through the town.

But now he walks the streets and he looks at all he meets, sad and wan.
And he shakes his feeble head and it seems as if he said, "They're gone."

My grandmama has said, poor old lady, she is dead long ago, that he had
a Roman nose and his cheek was like a rose in the snow.

But now his nose is thin, and it rests upon his chin like a staff. And a crook
is in his back and a melancholy crack is in his laugh.

I know it's a sin, for me to sit and grin at him here, but the old three-cornered hat and the britches and all that are so queer.

And if I should live to be the last leaf on the tree in the spring, let them smile as I do now at the old forsaken bough, where I cling.[32]

Is there a last leaf on the tree somewhere who needs a little encouragement from you today? Why not give him or her a call?

Full-Time Mothers

Let me ask, do you think it is appropriate for a woman, especially a college student, to make it her exclusive career goal to be a wife and mother? Or is that a waste of her talents? Most women's studies programs in large universities consider the choice of homemaking to be almost a betrayal.

I remember a senior who came to ask me about that issue. We talked about various job opportunities and the possibility of her going to graduate school. Then she suddenly paused, leaned toward me, and said almost in a whisper, "May I be completely honest with you?"

I said, "Sure, Julie. There's no one here but us. You can say anything you want."

"Well," she said in a hushed tone, "I don't want to have a career at all. What I really want is to be a full-time wife and mother."

I asked, "Why do you say it as though it's some kind of secret? It's your life. What's wrong with doing whatever you want?"

"Are you kidding?" she replied. "If my professors and my classmates at the university knew that's what I wanted, they'd laugh me out of school."

How unfortunate that a young woman should have to apologize for wanting to have babies and devote herself to their care for a few years. That way of life has been honored and respected for centuries, yet it has fallen into disrepute.

Not every woman chooses to be a full-time homemaker, of course. Some are more interested in a career, and that is certainly their prerogative. Others have no plans to marry. That's all right, too. But those who *do* elect to be stay-at-home moms should not be ashamed to admit it—even on a university campus.

Oh yes, and what about Julie? She has three beautiful teenagers now and still loves her job as a full-time mom. And why not, for Pete's sake?

The Battle of the Somme

Though the world has largely forgotten it, July 1 is the anniversary of one of the worst military catastrophes in human history. It is called the Battle of the Somme, and it took place in France during the First World War.

On that day the Allied commander, General Douglas Haig, foolishly ordered more than 100,000 men to charge across "no man's land" just after dawn. The German army knew that an attack was coming, and they crisscrossed the battlefield with machine-gun fire, systematically mowing down the heavily laden troops. It was the bloodiest day in British history, with nearly twenty thousand men killed and thirty-five thousand wounded. The French and German troops suffered comparable casualties.[33]

The tragedy of the Somme was its utter waste of human lives. The battle continued for 140 days and soon involved some 3 million men. More than a third of them became casualties before it was over. And for what? The Allies never drove the Germans back more than seven miles at any point, and even that ground was lost in 1918.[34]

Oh, I know this all happened long ago and far away. What does it matter today? But somehow it seems fitting for us to pause for a moment to remember the sacrifice of the men who died and the 4 million family members whose beloved husbands, sons, and fathers never returned. It all began at dawn on July 1, 1916.

The Little Girl in the Airport

You can learn a great deal by watching people, which happens to be one of my favorite pastimes. I was doing just that some years ago while waiting to catch a plane at Los Angeles International Airport. Standing near me was an old man, obviously waiting for a passenger who should have been on the plane that had just arrived. At his side was a little girl, who must have been about seven years old. She, too, was looking for a certain face in the crowd. She clung to the old man's arm, whom I assumed to have been her grandfather. They both seemed unusually stressed.

As the last passengers filed by, the girl began to cry. She wasn't merely disappointed in that moment; her little heart was broken. The grandfather also appeared to be fighting back tears. For some reason, he failed to comfort the child, who buried her face in the sleeve of his coat. I wondered what special agony they were going through. Was it the child's mother who failed to show up? Or had the little girl's daddy promised to come and then changed his mind?

The old man and the child waited for yet another plane and then gave up hope. The only sound was the sniffing of the little girl as they walked through the terminal and toward the door. When I last saw her, she was still clutching her grandfather's sleeve.

Where is that child now, who must be in her late twenties? God only knows. Somewhere out there is a young woman with a very bitter memory—one which I happened to have been there to witness.

Mom's Football Team

In the late 1960s, the phrase "If it feels good, do it" made its way around the counterculture. It meant, in effect, that a person's flighty impulses should be allowed to overrule every other consideration. "Don't think—just follow your heart" was the prevailing attitude. That foolish advice has ruined many gullible people. Those who ignore lurking dangers are casting themselves adrift in the path of life's storms. We must be prepared to disregard ephemeral feelings at times and govern our behavior with common sense.

Not only can emotions be dangerous—they can also be unreliable and foolish. I'm reminded of a story told by my mother about her high school years. They had one of the worst football teams in the history of Oklahoma. They hadn't won a game in years. Finally a wealthy oil producer asked to speak to the team in the locker room and offered a brand-new Ford to every boy and to each coach if they would simply defeat their bitter rivals in the next game. The team went crazy. For seven days they thought about nothing but football. They couldn't even sleep at night. Finally the big night arrived, and the team was frantic with anticipation. They assembled on the sidelines, put their hands together, and shouted, "Rah!" Then they ran onto the field—and were smashed thirty-eight to nothing. No amount of excitement could compensate for the players' lack of discipline, conditioning, practice, study, coaching, drill, experience, and character. Such is the nature of emotion. It has a definite place in human affairs but is not a substitute for intelligence, preparation, and self-control.

Instead of responding to your impulses, therefore, it is often better to hang tough when you feel like quitting, to guard your tongue when you feel like talking, to save your money when you feel like spending, and to remain faithful when you feel like flirting. Unbridled feelings will get you in trouble nine times out of ten.

So, before you chase after something that simply feels good, you might want to think it over. You could be about to make one of your greatest blunders.

Dishonest Emotions

I had a friend who won a Bronze Star for courage in Vietnam. But the first night his unit arrived on the battlefield, he and the other men were scared to death. They dug foxholes and nervously watched the sun disappear beyond the horizon. At approximately midnight, the enemy attacked with a vengeance. Before long, all the soldiers were firing frantically and throwing hand grenades in the darkness. The battle raged throughout the night, and the troops appeared to be winning. At last the sun came up, and the body count began. But not one dead Vietcong soldier lay at the perimeter of the mountain. In fact, no enemy had ever been there. The nervous troops had imagined the entire attack.

The reaction of the men was typical of frightened people of any age. The mind will generate evidence to validate anxieties. A person who fears cancer, for example, will sometimes develop all the telltale symptoms even though no disease process is there. And a child who awakens at night will "hear" scary sounds echoing through the house. That's just the way our emotions work. So before you panic, cool down a bit. The danger might be, and probably is, imaginary. . . .

Inveterate Liars

We've been discussing the nature of human emotions and how they distort reality. Here's another example: The city of Los Angeles was paralyzed with fear in 1969 when Charles Manson and his "family" murdered many people in cold blood. Residents wondered who would be next. My mother was quite convinced that she was the prime candidate. Sure enough, Mom and Dad heard the intruder as they lay in bed one night.

Thump came the sound from the area of the kitchen.

"Did you hear that?" asked my mother.

"Yes, be quiet," said my father.

They lay staring into the darkness, breathing shallowly and listening for further clues. A second *thump* brought them to their feet. They felt their way to the bedroom door, which was closed. Mom propped her foot against the door and threw her weight against the upper section. My father characteristically wanted to confront the attacker head-on. He reached through the darkness and grasped the doorknob, but his pull met the resistance from my mother. Dad assumed someone was holding the door from the other side, while my mother could feel the killer trying to force it open.

My parents stood there in the blackness, struggling against one another and imagining themselves to be in a tug-of-war with a killer. Finally Mother ran to the window to scream, which allowed Dad to open the door. That's when she noticed that the light was on in the hall. In reality, no prowler was there. The thumps were never identified, and Charles Manson never made his anticipated visit.

This story illustrates the way fearful people can be deceived by human emotions. Feelings are inveterate liars that often confirm our worst fears.

That's why I wrote a book whose title asked this question, Emotions: can you trust them? It took me two hundred pages to say no!

Bees and Flies

I heard recently about an experiment in which twelve bees were placed in a jar in a darkened room. A light was beamed onto the bottom of the glass, and then the lid was removed. Instinctively, the bees flew toward the light and couldn't escape. All of the bees died trying to buzz their way through the bottom of the jar.

Next the researchers took twelve common house flies and repeated the experiment. Within seconds the flies had found their way out of the jar. It is known that bees are more intelligent than flies, and their survival instincts are usually better defined. Yet it was those very instincts that doomed the bees.[35]

I wonder how often our own preconceived notions get in the way of common sense? My father, for example, hated automatic transmissions on automobiles because he learned to drive with stick shifts. I've fallen into similar patterns. Until 1992 I wrote books with pencils on yellow pads. I did that for years after word processors were available. The twentieth century was almost over before I decided to join it.

Rigidity and the force of habit can also cause us to do things that make no sense. What illogical ideas are you holding onto these days? It's a question worth pondering.

Legend of the Taj Mahal

The Taj Mahal is one of the most beautiful and costly tombs ever built, but there is something fascinating about its beginnings.

In 1629, when the favorite wife of Indian ruler Shah Jahan died, he ordered that a magnificent tomb be built as a memorial to her. The shah placed his wife's casket in the middle of a parcel of land, and construction of the temple literally began around it. But several years into the venture, the Shah's grief for his wife gave way to a passion for the project. One day while he was surveying the sight, he reportedly stumbled over a wooden box, and he had some workers throw it out. It was months before he realized that his wife's casket had been destroyed. The original purpose for the memorial became lost in the details of construction.[36]

This legend may or may not be true, but its theme is a familiar one in the lives of people. How many of us set out to build dream castles but lose our focus along the way? We realize too late that it is loved ones and our children that really matter.

Another classic example of misplaced values occurred in the life of J. Paul Getty, one of the richest men of this century. He wrote: "I've never been given to envy, save for the envy I feel toward those people who have the ability to make a marriage work and endure happily. It's an art I've never been able to master."[37]

While we're building our Taj Mahals, let's not forget the purpose with which we began building.[38]

Blended Families

I want to offer a word or two of advice to those who are planning to remarry after divorce or the death of a spouse. When children are involved, this is called a blended family, and it poses some very unique and unsettling challenges.

I can tell you that the Brady Bunch is a myth—the notion that a mom and dad with six kids can create one big happy family without conflict or rivalries. It just doesn't happen that way, although many blended families do eventually adjust to their new circumstances. Initially, at least, it is common within a blended family for one or more kids to see the new stepparent as a usurper. Their loyalty to the memory of their departed mother or father can be intense. For them to welcome a newcomer with open arms would be an act of betrayal. This places the stepparent in an impossible bind.

It is also common for one child to move into the power vacuum left by the departing parent. That youngster becomes the surrogate spouse.

I'm not referring to sexual matters. Rather, that boy or girl begins relating to the remaining parent more as a peer. The status and power that come with that supportive role are very seductive, and a youngster can be unwilling to give them up.

These are only two of the land mines that can threaten blended families. Unfortunately there are others.

The Second Time Around

We've discussed blended families and the special challenges they typically face. But there is a more serious problem that can develop. It concerns the way the new husband and wife feel about their kids. Each is irrationally committed to his or her own flesh and blood, while being merely acquainted with the others. When fights and insults occur between the two sets of children, parents are almost always partial to those they brought into the world. It is natural for their allegiance to be directed to their own kids. Unfortunately, this creates a tendency for the blended family to dissolve into armed camps—us against them. If the kids sense this tension between parents, some will exploit it to gain power over siblings.

Some terrible battles can occur unless there are some ways to ventilate these feelings. Given the challenges, it is apparent why the probabilities of second and third marriages' being successful are considerably lower than the first.

It is possible to blend families successfully, of course, and millions of people have done it. But the task *is* difficult, and you may need some help in pulling it off. That's why I strongly suggest that those planning to remarry seek professional counseling as early as possible. It is expensive, but another divorce is even more costly.

Robin in a Rainstorm

single mother sent a story to me recently that helped explain the loneliness and stress faced by those who are raising their children alone. She said she was looking out her window one drizzly day, and she saw an unfolding drama. A mother robin and her brood of chicks were perched in the nest of a scrub-oak tree. As the rain poured down, the mother bird covered her chirping little chicks beneath her extended wings. Then the hail began to fall. Instead of tucking her head safely in the nest, the mother robin raised her head upward and took the blows to protect her young. All of the chicks made it safely through the storm.

What a graphic illustration of the perils of single parenting! That responsibility of raising kids alone is unrelenting, requiring moms and dads to earn a living, cook, clean, supervise homework, take care of sick kids, etcetera. Beyond these day by day duties, they must figure out how to meet their own personal and spiritual needs. Taken in context, this may be one of the toughest assignments on earth. Single parents, whether mothers or fathers, need our continued support and prayers.

To those who are taking the blows on behalf of their children, let me assure you that a better day is coming. The storm won't last forever. A beautiful rainbow will soon appear. And when the job has been completed and a brood of healthy little birds has been raised, there will be sweet benefits for the parents who don't fly away.

Perseverance

A braham Lincoln was perhaps the greatest of all U.S. presidents. He led the nation through its darkest hour, preserved the union, and issued the historic Emancipation Proclamation. What is equally impressive, however, is the way he handled adversity.

You may have heard about his many disappointments and failures, but perhaps your children haven't. Let me cite the record again in memory of this great man. In 1831 he suffered a business failure. In 1832 he was defeated in a bid for the state legislature. In 1833 he underwent a second business failure. In 1835 his fiancée died. In 1836 he experienced a mental breakdown. In 1838 he was defeated for speaker of the state legislature. In 1840 he was defeated for the office of elector. In 1843 he was defeated for land officer. In 1846 he won an election for the Congress. But in 1848 he was defeated in his reelection bid. In 1855 he was defeated in a run for the Senate. In 1856 he was defeated in his bid for vice president. In 1858 he lost again in another attempt at the Senate, and in 1860 he was elected president of the United States.[39]

What incredible perseverance in the face of adversity! It is a lesson in history that every schoolchild should be taught to appreciate.

Heaven's Gate

You might remember the tragic account of the Heaven's Gate cult whose thirty-nine members committed suicide in 1997. Their expectation of boarding a spaceship left the American people shocked and puzzled. What would cause so many seemingly healthy people to kill themselves in pursuit of a fantasy from outer space?

The cult might have been motivated unconsciously by the quest for significance and purpose that resides within the human spirit. To satisfy that search for meaning, each of us must answer numerous questions posed by life, including "Who am I?" "Why do I exist?" "Who created me?" and "Is there life after death?" People who are unable to find satisfactory answers to these questions become sitting ducks for the con men of our time. They often chase after crazy notions cooked up by gurus and self-appointed saviors, who tell lies to those who *need* to believe.

Someone explained it this way: "Superstition is the worm that exudes from the grave of a dead faith." In other words, when a person recognizes no god who can give meaning to life, there is a great void inside that aches to be filled. Frequently that individual will turn to hocus-pocus, magic, UFOs, and ancient myths to satisfy his or her deep longings. It would appear that the Heaven's Gate cult succumbed to that false teaching.

There is a lesson worth noting here for parents. We simply must give our children something in which to believe—not just *something,* but the *only* true source of Truth in the person of Jesus Christ. The failure to accomplish that quest for meaning can leave them vulnerable to bizarre cults. In regard to the Heaven's Gate cult, it sent thirty-nine people to their deaths while trying to flag down a passing spaceship.

The Hallway of Doors

I magine, if you will, a long dark hallway with a series of doors on either side. Written on each door is the name of an addiction, such as alcohol, tobacco, marijuana, hard drugs, gambling, pornography, etc. Now, teenagers must walk down the hallway on this journey from childhood to adulthood. The temptation is very great to open one or more of the doors along the way. They can hear the beat of the music and the raucous laughter of their friends echoing from inside. The pressure to join them can be enormous. And it is very difficult to convince a fun-loving adolescent that he or she should stay in the dark hallway, which seems so boring and embarrassing.

Unfortunately, for a certain percentage of individuals who open one or more of these dangerous doors, a tragedy begins to unfold. If a person is susceptible—and there's no way to know in advance—he or she only has to crack the door an inch or two and a monster will run out and grab that young man or woman. Some will be held in its grip for the rest of their lives.

If you talk to an alcoholic about his or her addiction, you'll learn that it probably began casually—with no hint that life was about to take a radical and tragic turn. It all started with the opening of a door—probably during the teen years.

Talking to a Teen

There are some teenagers who sail right through the adolescent experience with hardly any evidence of turbulence. They make wonderful grades in school; they're a delight to their teachers and a treasure to their parents. But there are others, as we all know, who seem to declare war on the world and stay mad for the next ten years.

Mark Twain was referring to this second kind of kid when he wrote, "When a child turns 12, you should put him in a barrel, nail a lid down and feed him through a knot hole. When he turns 16, you should seal up the knot hole."[40] There are times when parents have reason to feel that way, to be sure.

Erma Bombeck said she wasn't going to pay two thousand dollars to straighten the teeth of a kid who never smiled. Another mother talked about how her son had been a chatterbox throughout childhood, but when he became a teenager, his vocabulary consisted of only nine word-phrases. They were "I dunno," "Maybe," "I forget," "Huh?" "No!" "Nope," "Yeah," "Who—me?" and "He did it."

Well, what are you going to do if your sweet, cuddly, cooperative preteen-ager turns into a sullen, silent adolescent? The answer is, you go right on loving him or her. What is going on inside that youngster, hormonally and emotionally, explains much of what you see on the outside. But it won't always be that way. Better days are coming. The smile and a rich vocabulary will return. I promise.

Depressed Children

We used to believe that only adults suffered from depression, but that understanding is changing. Now we're seeing signs of serious despondency in children as young as five years old.

Symptoms of depression in an elementary schoolchild may include general lethargy, a lack of interest in things that used to excite him or her, sleep disturbances, chewed fingernails, loss of appetite, and violent emotional outbursts. Stomach complaints can be another tip-off, as well as an intolerance to frustration.

If you suspect that your child is beginning to show the signs of depression, you should help him or her verbalize feelings. Try to anticipate the explanation for sadness or anger, and lead the youngster into conversations that provide an opportunity to ventilate. Make yourself available to listen without judging or belittling the feelings expressed. Simply being understood is soothing for children and adults alike.

If the problem persists, I urge you to seek professional help. Prolonged depression can be destructive for human beings of any age, and it is especially dangerous to children.

Bill and Frank

One of the most powerful stories in the history of the Olympic Games involved a canoeing specialist named Bill Havens. He was a shoe-in, I'm told, to win a gold medal in the 1924 Olympic Games in Paris.

But a few months before the Games were held, he learned that his wife would likely give birth to their first child while he was away. She told him that she could make it on her own, but this was a milestone Bill just didn't want to miss. So he surprised everyone and stayed home. Bill greeted his infant son, Frank, into the world on August 1, 1924. Though he always wondered what might have been, he said he never regretted his decision.

Well, he poured his life into that little lad and shared with him a love for the rapids. Twenty-four years passed, and the Olympic Games were held in Helsinki, Finland. This time Frank Havens was chosen to compete in the canoeing event. The day after the competition, Bill received a telegram from his son that read: "Dear Dad, Thanks for waiting around for me to be born in 1924. I'm coming home with the gold medal that you should have won." It was signed, "Your loving son, Frank."[41]

Many would question Bill Haven's decision to miss his big opportunity in Paris, but he never wavered. He wanted his family to know that they always came first, no matter what. And that made him a hero to a little boy named Frank.

Going Down for the Third Time

When my wife, Shirley, and I were first married, we took a weekend trip to a local resort. She quickly put on her swimsuit and jumped into the pool before I could get there. She was surrounded by sunbathers and muscular lifeguards, who sat basking in the sun.

Shirley is not a strong swimmer and began to tire as she reached the deep end of the pool. The more she flailed at the water, the more exhausted she became. She began to be seized by panic.

I'm going to drown! she thought. *There's no way I can make it.*

All Shirley had to do was scream for help and the lifeguards and sixteen male swimmers would have been at her side. But to do so would have embarrassed her in front of all those gorgeous sunbathers. She decided to risk drowning rather than humiliate herself. Fortunately, she managed to splash her way to the edge, clinging there coughing, sputtering, and gasping for air.

That story reminds me of the people who are going under but are still unwilling to call for help. Some are alcoholics, who deny they have a problem. Some are teenage druggies, who can't admit they are hooked. Some even commit suicide rather than reach for the help that is readily available.

If you're drowning in a deep pool, call for help. Don't let your pride take you to the bottom.

Shakespeare and Me

How do you teach basic honesty to kids? Well, I can tell you how my mother did it. When I was in the eighth grade, I was required to read a certain number of great books during the first semester. Like most fourteen-year-olds, however, I had other things on my mind.

I still hadn't begun the assignment as we approached the end of the term—so I selected the thickest, heaviest books in the library and told my teacher I had read them all. Consequently, she gave me an A+ on my report card. My mom was impressed, my dad was proud, and I was as guilty as sin.

In a moment of true confession, I admitted to my mother that I had cheated. Instead of getting mad at me or grounding me for six years, she simply said, quietly but with intensity, "Well, you'll just have to read the books."

"But, Mom," I said, "how can I read the collected works of William Shakespeare, *Ben Hur,* and about ten other huge books?"

"I don't know," she said, "but you're gonna do it." I spent the rest of that school year poring over the classics, while my friends played football and talked to girls outside my window. I'll tell you, it was grueling. No one ever paid more dearly for a little dishonesty. When the task was finally done, I went to my teacher and tearfully confessed the entire scam. She forgave me and let me rejoin the human race.

I never forgot that lesson in accountability, as painful as it was. But I'm glad the lady of the house didn't let me off the hook. She was too smart for that!

Sheep Led to Slaughter

I once saw a dramatic documentary film that featured a packing-house where sheep were slaughtered. Huddled in pens were hundreds of nervous animals that seemed to sense danger in their unfamiliar surroundings. Then a gate was opened leading to a ramp and through a door to the right. In order to get the sheep to walk up that ramp, the workers used what is known as a "Judas goat." This is a goat that has been trained to lead the sheep into the slaughterhouse.

The goat confidently walked to the bottom of the ramp and looked back. Then he took a few more steps and stopped again. The sheep looked at each other skittishly and began moving toward the ramp. Eventually, they followed the confident goat to the top, where he went through another gate that closed behind him. This forced the sheep directly into the slaughterhouse. It was a dramatic illustration of herd behavior with deadly consequences.

There is a striking similarity between the sheep following the Judas goat and teenagers who succumb to peer pressure. Those who are more confident and rebellious often lead the timid into trouble. Some inject themselves with heroin or get involved with cocaine; others engage in dangerous sexual practices, such as driving while drinking and engaging in violent behavior. But why do they do such destructive things? Don't they care about their own lives and the future they are risking? Most of them do. But the pressure to conform—to follow the Judas goat—is even stronger than the need for security and well-being.

Adults have a similar problem. The prophet Isaiah observed it when he wrote, "We all, like sheep, have gone astray."[42]

Steroid Madness

A new threat to the health of young female athletes has come to light. A study published in the *Archives of Pediatric and Adolescent Medicine* has revealed that high school girls are using anabolic steroids in greater numbers than previously known.

With the opportunity for college scholarships and even professional sports careers for women, the incentives to build more muscle are irresistible to some teenagers—and perhaps even to their parents. Steroids are also used to help them achieve the "lean" look idealized by the entertainment and fashion industries. Whatever the motivation, three national surveys confirmed that 175,000 American high school females, or 2.4 percent, say they have used steroids at least once. Twice as many boys have experimented with the drugs, but until now it was believed that usage was rare among girls.

Please listen to this, parents: Lifelong physical problems befall those who take steroids. For girls, it can mean a general masculinization of features, including male hair growth, deepening of the voice, shrinkage of the breasts, and menstrual problems. These effects are permanent, like a tattoo that will be with them forever. More serious problems, including liver, cardiovascular, and reproductive illnesses, are also common.[43]

The bottom line is this: Steroid usage is disastrous for females as well as for males.

Little Ears

Parents need to be very careful about comments made within hearing of their children. Youngsters are often very capable of understanding and remembering insulting remarks. When I was five years old, for example, I came running into a room just in time to hear my father say something unkind to several other men. I still recall that remark made many years ago. My dad didn't intend to hurt me through his insensitivity to others, and he later apologized. But his carelessness became part of the permanent record in my mind.

I've heard similar mistakes made by parents seeking my advice after a speaking engagement. They would begin talking openly with me about a problem one of their kids was having. As they described an embarrassing characteristic, I would notice that the kids were standing by their moms and listening intently. They may never forget insulting comments made in their hearing.

Surprisingly, it's not just insensitive parents who make such blunders.

I once referred to a neurologist a bright, nine-year-old boy, who was having a severe learning problem. After giving the lad a thorough examination, the neurologist invited the parents and their son into the office for a consultation. Then he diagnosed the "brain damage" in front of the wide-eyed little patient as though he couldn't hear those awesome words or comprehend their implications. I'm certain the child never forgot them.

Sensitivity is the key. It means tuning in to the thoughts and feelings of our kids during their vulnerable years.

The Captain and the Seaman

In the official magazine of the Naval Institute, Frank Koch reported on a very unusual encounter at sea.

A battleship was coming in for maneuvers in heavy weather. Shortly after the sun went down, the lookout reported a light in the distance, so the captain had the signalman send a message: "We're on a collision course. Advise you to change your course twenty degrees."

Minutes later a signal came back: "Advisable for you to change your course."

The captain angrily ordered that another signal be sent: "I am a captain. Change course twenty degrees."

Again came the reply: "I'm a seaman, second class. You'd better change your course."

Furious by this point, the captain barked a final threat. "I'm a battleship! Change your course!"

The signal came back. "I'm a lighthouse."

The captain changed his course![44]

I don't care how big and powerful a person may become, it's foolhardy to ignore the beacons that warn us of danger. They take various forms: symptoms of health problems, prolonged marital conflict, rebellious children, excessive debt, stress that ties us in knots. These are the warning signs of approaching danger. It matters not that we're successful, influential, and busy. A seaman, second class, sits in a lighthouse somewhere and signals, "Change your course," and the wise captain does so with haste.

Needle Park

Perhaps you've noted that some legislators are again toying with the idea of legalizing drugs and offering free needle-exchange programs. The idea is to slow the spread of AIDS and to take the profit out of the drug business. Their argument is seductive, but it is dangerous in my view.

Before such programs are initiated, officials should review the experience of the Swiss. In the late 1980s they set aside city property where addicts could legally shoot up and where free needles were provided, no questions asked. The area of Platzspitz became known as "Needle Park," and it went terribly wrong. Before long, the number of druggies visiting the park soared from two hundred to twenty thousand.[45]

Ten thousand "consumption events" occurred per day, as users from all over Switzerland came to get in on the fun. They soon outnumbered even the local population. The death rate rose as health officials sought to resuscitate as many as forty-five overdose cases per day. And, as should have been expected, the crime rate went through the roof.

City officials finally called off the experiment and closed the park. Almost immediately the crime rate dropped to its former levels, and the program ended in total failure.[46] Even if the plan had worked, it sent this message to kids: "Don't use drugs, but here's what you'll need to do it."

There has to be a better answer than this to one of the greatest curses of our time. I hope our decision makers won't make the same blunder!

The Shy Child

I heard about a twelve-year-old boy who had never spoken a word in his life. His parents and his siblings thought he couldn't talk because they'd never heard his voice. Then one day the boy's mother placed a bowl of soup in front of him, and he took one spoonful. He pushed it away and said, "This is slop! I won't eat any more of it!"

The family was ecstatic. The boy had actually spoken a complete sentence! The father jumped up gleefully and said, "Why haven't you ever talked to us before?"

"Because," the boy said, "up until now, everything's been OK."

There are many shy kids among us who just don't do much talking. When they meet new people, they stand with their tongues in their cheeks and look down as though they're ashamed. Their parents wish they would be more assertive.

The question is, why are these kids so introverted and withdrawn? The answer is that they're born that way. According to the New York

Longitudinal Study, shyness occurs in about 15 percent of children and tends to be a lifelong characteristic.[47] It is a function of heredity and temperament.

You can teach the social graces to a shy child, but it isn't wise to tamper with the basic personality. Instead, accept him or her exactly as designed. There's not another child on earth quite like that unique individual.

The Straight Life

If we are to believe the findings of behavioral researchers, extramarital affairs are more common now than ever in the United States. People who ought to know better, such as ministers, physicians, and politicians, are risking marriages, careers, and children to engage in sexual misconduct. Even the president of the United States has participated in one or more dalliances that have jeopardized his place in history. Immoral behavior of this nature is destroying millions of families at every level of society.

The question I would pose is this: What happens to individuals who cheat on their spouses—those who leave the "straight life" in pursuit of someone more exciting?

I have watched such people over the years, and what I've observed is that they eventually establish another "straight life." After the thrill of the chase and the cooling of passion, folks have to get back to cooking, cleaning, and earning a living. The grass is greener on the other side of the fence, but it still has to be mowed. Also, personal flaws and irritants show up, much like those in the former husband or wife. And guess what? The straight life begins to feel confining again. Then what does the individual do when he or she is beginning to feel trapped? Some people then hopscotch from one straight life to another in a vain search for something indescribable—something they never seem to find. Lying in their wake are former spouses, who feel rejected, bitter, and unloved. They produce vulnerable little children, who wonder why Daddy doesn't live here anymore and why Mommy cries all the time.

Soaps and sitcoms on television tell us every day that infidelity is a marvelous game for two. It sure does look like fun. But when adultery has run its course, it only brings pain and disillusionment. And the ones who are hurt the most are the children who are caught in the web.

Temperaments and Kids

L et's talk today about two kinds of children who are seen in every school classroom.

Those in the first category are by nature rather organized boys and girls (more girls than boys) who care about details. They take the learning process very seriously and assume full responsibility for assignments given. To do poorly on a test would depress them for several days. Parents of these children don't have to monitor their progress to keep them working; it is their way of life, and it is consistent with their temperaments.

The second category of children includes the boys and girls (more boys than girls) who just don't fit in with the structure of the classroom. They're sloppy, disorganized, and flighty. They have a natural aversion to work, and they love to play. They can't wait for success, so they hurry on without it. Like bacteria that gradually become immune to antibiotics, the classic underachievers become impervious to adult pressure. They withstand a storm of parental protest every few weeks, and then when no one's looking, they slip back into apathy. They don't even hear the assignments being given in school, and they seem not to be embarrassed in the least when they fail to complete them. If they graduate at all, it's not gonna be cum laude; it'll be "thank you laudy."

We really should talk more about these disorganized children because God sure made a lot of them. They drive their parents to distraction, and their unwillingness to work can turn their homes into World War III. I'll offer some suggestions that may be helpful in another commentary.

Go with the Flow

We talked last time about the flighty, disorganized children who absolutely refuse to do assigned schoolwork. Let me share some additional thoughts about underachieving children.

First, these kids are not intrinsically inferior to their hardworking siblings. Yes, it would be wonderful if all students used their talents to best advantage. But children are unique individuals, and they don't have to fit the same mold. Besides, the classic underachievers sometimes outperform the academic superstars in the long run. That's what happened to Einstein, Edison, Eleanor Roosevelt, and others. So don't write off that disorganized, apparently lazy kid as a lifelong loser. He or she may surprise you.

Second, you will never turn an underachieving youngster into a scholar by nagging, pushing, threatening, and punishing. It just isn't in him. If you try to squeeze him into something he's not, you will only aggravate the child and frustrate yourself.

Third, stay as close as possible to the school. Your restless child isn't going to tell you what's going on there, so you need to find out for yourself. And seek tutorial assistance, if necessary, to keep him on track.

Fourth, your child lacks the discipline to structure his life. Help him generate it.

Finally, having done what you can to help, accept what he does in return. Go with the flow, and begin looking for other areas of success for your child. That advice will be best for your son or daughter and, I assure you, much easier on your nerves, too!

Talking Scale

A few years ago, my staff bought me a "talking scale" for my birthday. I never told them how badly I hated that thing. It had no volume control and shouted my weight all over the neighborhood. Nevertheless, I went on a two-week diet shortly thereafter and used the scale to monitor my weight loss. Every morning I would get out of bed and climb on board, to which a man's voice would respond by giving me the good (or bad) news.

About twelve days later I hopped on the scale one morning, and it promptly told me I weighed 278 pounds. I couldn't have gained eighty pounds in one day, so I got off and back on again. This time it said, "Your weight is 147 pounds." Every time I stepped on the scale, it reported a different number. Why had it suddenly gone bonkers?

Finally, I stepped up again, and the crazy thing didn't say anything. I stood there in my pajamas, feeling stupid and waiting for this cuckoo machine to talk to me. After a long pause, a very tired voice said, "Myyyyyy baaatterreez aaarrrrrrr loooooooow."

I said, "I know buddy. So are mine."

I'll bet I'm writing for someone today who is suffering from that chronic illness known as "low batteries." The best cure for a power failure is a radical change of pace—even if it's only for a day or two. Take off. Get out. Play hooky. Go shopping. Do something that you've been wanting to do, just for fun.

Then, perhaps, you'll come home with your batteries recharged and raring to go.

Infant Mortality

P eter Brimelow, writing in a recent issue of *Forbes,* described the terrible curse of maternal and infant mortality during the eighteenth and nineteenth centuries.

Death in that era came calling at nearly every door, whether humble or proud. In the 1700s one baby in five died in infancy, and thirty-three mothers out of every one thousand were lost in childbirth. Abraham Lincoln suffered the loss of a child in infancy, and a well-known minister, Cotton Mather, buried eight of his children before their second birthdays.

As for the deaths of mothers in that era, it may be difficult for us to understand today just what that meant to the families, but it was usually devastating. It wasn't uncommon for a woman with eight or ten children to die during yet another delivery, leaving a grief-stricken father to raise his kids while continuing the exhausting tasks of farming or ranching. The rate of infant and maternal mortality remained terribly high well into the modern era. Given this history, we have much to be thankful for today. The current death rate for mothers in childbirth is only one in 14,285 and for babies only one in 1,400.[48]

It is appropriate that we pause today to acknowledge the remarkable achievements of medical science and to tip our hats to the men and women who continue to make pregnancy and childbirth a relatively safe experience.

Ride down the Rogue

Many years ago my family and I took a raft trip down the Rogue River in Oregon. It almost became my last ride. After floating serenely for two days, I was suddenly thrown into the turbulent river. It seemed like an eternity before I came to the surface, only to discover I couldn't breathe. A bandanna that had been wrapped around my neck was now plastered across my mouth and held there by my glasses, which were strapped to my head. Just as I clawed free and gasped for air, churning water hit me in the face and gurgled into my lungs. I definitely considered the possibility that I was drowning. Fortunately, I managed to pull myself back into the raft, where I lay sucking air for about twenty minutes.

I've thought often about that experience in the ensuing years and concluded that life often resembles that beautiful Rogue River. There are long stretches when the water is calm and serene. You can see your reflection as you lean out of the raft. The scenery is gorgeous, and the river carries you peacefully downstream. Then without warning you are thrown overboard and taken to the bottom. Suddenly, you're gasping for air and thinking you're going to drown for sure.

It would be helpful for young people to know that this *will* happen to them sooner or later. No one travels down the river of life without encountering the rapids. There will be moments of serenity and beauty. But there will also be times of sheer terror when they'll be at the mercy of the good Lord.

It's all part of the ride.

Bundy's Last Words

In 1989 I conducted a videotaped interview with Ted Bundy just a few hours before he was to be executed for killing at least twenty-eight women and girls. During that candid conversation in the shadow of the electric chair, Bundy described how he had come to be addicted to pornography since finding detective magazines in a dump when he was thirteen years of age. He was later obsessed by violent images that led to the murders of many women and a twelve-year-old girl. After spending twelve years on death row and meeting many killers, Bundy became convinced that pornography has a horrible effect on men, who are particularly susceptible to it. He argued passionately, there in the last hours of his life, for additional limits on the sale and distribution of obscene materials.

This is a portion of Bundy's last words:

I can only hope that those who I have harmed and those who I have caused so much grief—even if they don't believe my expression of sorrow and remorse—will believe what I'm saying now, that there is loose in their towns, in their communities, people like me today whose dangerous impulses are being fueled day in and day out by violence in the media in its various forms, particularly sexualized violence. . . . And what scares and appalls me, Dr. Dobson, is . . . when I see what's on cable TV, some of the movies, some of the violence in the movies that come into homes today [is] stuff that they wouldn't [have showed] in X-rated adult theaters thirty years ago. . . . But I'll tell you, there are lots of other kids playing in streets around this country today who are going to be dead tomorrow and the next day and the next day and next month, because other young people are reading the kinds of things and seeing the kinds of things that are available in the media today.[49]

I am certain that Bundy was right. Every few days we read about another boy or girl who has been sexually assaulted and brutally murdered. When a suspect is identified, authorities typically find boxes of pornography in his possession, much of it depicting violence against women and children. It has become a very familiar pattern.

Families at the Dinner Table

D r. Blake Bowden and his colleagues at the Cincinnati Children's Hospital Center studied 527 teenagers to learn what family and lifestyle characteristics were related to mental health and adjustment. Their findings were significant.

What they found is that adolescents whose parents ate dinner with them five times per week or more were the least likely to be on drugs, to be depressed, or to be in trouble with the law. They were more likely to be doing well in school and to be surrounded by a supportive circle of friends. Surprisingly, the benefit was seen even for families that didn't eat together at home. Those who met at fast-food restaurants had the same result. By contrast, the more poorly adjusted teens ate with their parents only three evenings per week or less.

What do these findings mean? Is there something magic about sitting down together over a meal? No, and those parents who interpret the conclusions that way will be disappointed. What Bowden's study shows is that adolescents do far better in school and in life when their parents are *involved* with them—when they have time for them—and specifically, when they get together almost every day for conversation and interaction.[50]

Study after study has emphasized that same message. Families are critically important to the well-being of children.

Barbie and Her Pals

Many years ago I wrote in one of my books that I didn't like what Barbie dolls did to little girls who played with them. Parents still ask why I feel that way.

Let me begin by admitting that my daughter played with Barbie dolls for years, despite my own views on this subject. I just didn't have the heart to take them away from her. Nevertheless, I *wished* Barbie would go away. There could be no better method for teaching the worship of beauty and materialism than is modeled by these dolls. If we intentionally sought to drill our little girls on the necessity of growing up rich and gorgeous, we could do no better than has already been done.

Did you ever see an ugly Barbie doll? Has she ever had even the slightest imperfection? No chance! She oozes femininity and sex appeal. Her hair is thick and gleaming—loaded with "body" (whatever that is). Her airbrushed skin is without flaw or blemish (except for a little statement on her bottom that says she was "Made in Hong Kong"). Such an idealized image creates later pressures when a real-life thirteen-year-old takes her first long look in the mirror. No doubt about it—Barbie she ain't!

In short, I'm philosophically opposed to these dolls primarily because they establish unrealistic expectations in years to come. That's my first concern. I'll share the second in my next commentary.

Teenie Barbies

I've discussed my concerns about Barbie dolls and their impact on little girls who become absorbed with them. They create an image of physical perfection that most girls will never be able to meet. I'm convinced that many self-image problems in the teen years are linked to a standard of beauty that is emphasized throughout childhood.

There is another concern that worries me. Barbie dolls (and their many competitors) usher girls into adolescent experiences long before they are ready for them. Instead of three- and four-year-old girls playing with stuffed animals, balls, cars, model horses, and the traditional memorabilia of childhood, they are learning to fantasize about life as a teenager. Barbie and her boyfriend, Ken, go on dates, learn to dance, drive expensive sports cars, get suntans, take camping trips, exchange marriage vows, and have babies (hopefully in that order). The entire adolescent culture, with its emphasis on sexual awareness, is illustrated to very young girls, who ought to be thinking about more childish things. This places them on an unnatural timetable likely to reach the peak of sexual interest several years before it is due—with all the obvious implications for their social and emotional health.

Regardless of what you do with Barbie and her gorgeous buddies, I strongly recommend that you postpone the adolescent experience until your children get there. They will have plenty of time afterward to be bona fide teenagers.

For Better or for Worse

My friends Keith and Mary Korstjens have been married for more than forty years. Shortly after their honeymoon, Mary was stricken with polio and became a quadriplegic. The doctors informed her that she would be confined to a wheelchair for the rest of her life. It was a devastating development, but Keith never wavered in his commitment to Mary. For all these years, he has bathed and dressed her, carried her to and from her bed, taken her to the bathroom, brushed her teeth, and combed her hair.

Obviously, Keith could have divorced Mary in 1957 and looked for a new and healthier wife, but he never even considered it. I admire this man, not only for doing the right thing, but for continuing to love and cherish his wife. Though the problems you and I face may be less challenging than those encountered by the Korstjens family, all of us will have our own difficulties. How will we respond? Some will give up on marriage for some pretty flimsy reasons. If we are going to go the distance, nothing short of an ironclad commitment will sustain us when the hard times come.

Let's review the vows spoken by millions during their marriage ceremonies. They read: "For better or for worse, for richer or for poorer, in sickness and in health, to love and to cherish, forsaking all others, from this day forward 'til death do us part." Keith and Mary Korstjens said and meant *exactly* that!

Forgiveness in Paducah

You probably remember the tragedy in the small town of Paducah, Kentucky. A fourteen-year-old boy named Michael Carneal opened fire on a group of students who had gathered in prayer. Within seconds, ten of them had been wounded, three of them fatally.

Who is this Michael Carneal, and what do we know about his earlier years? Well, he wasn't into drugs, crime, or cults. He was a solid B student who seldom got into trouble—either in school or at home. Still, there were signs. The theme of his school essays revealed that he felt "small and powerless." Friends say he was always angry about being teased in school. That has become a familiar pattern among those who commit acts of unprovoked violence.

While we need to understand more about Michael, I'm more interested in the other young men and women of Paducah. These kids showed a remarkable willingness to forgive. Placards began appearing at the high school reading We Forgive You, Mike. Kelly Carneal, Michael's sister, was not only embraced by her peers but also asked to sing in the choir at the slain girls' funeral. And during the town's annual Christmas parade, a moment of silent prayer was lifted up on behalf of Michael and his family.

One young girl said it best, "I can hate Michael and bear the scars of what he did for the rest of my life. But I choose to forgive him and get beyond it."[51]

What impressive maturity from teenagers under fire.

A Little Bit Helps

Have you noticed that most fitness fanatics are in their early twenties and in the bloom of health? They're not the ones primarily in need of exercise. It's us older folks who need help. Unfortunately, most of us in our forties, fifties, and sixties don't want to move unless absolutely necessary. One woman told me she had made a lifelong commitment not to sweat. Another lady said the only reason for jogging is to look better at her funeral. And a driver put this bumper sticker on his car: I'm pushing 50, and that's exercise enough.

For those who dislike jogging or pumping weights, let me offer some good news. A recent medical study found that it doesn't take much activity to improve general health and vastly reduce the risk of a fatal heart attack. An investigation conducted at the University of Minnesota revealed that work done around the house is sufficient to yield dramatic benefits. The researchers found that men and women who spent an average of forty-seven minutes a day on household chores, such as mowing the lawn, gardening, or just puttering around the house, enjoyed greater longevity than those who were inactive. It's even better if you do some push-ups and sit-ups every few days, but not necessary.[52]

So put down the remote control, get off the couch, and do a little home cleanup or repair. Not only will your house look better, but you're likely to live longer if you do.

A Great Father

S omeone has said, "Link a boy to the right man, and he will seldom go wrong." That adage is even more true when the "right man" happens to be his dad.

The influence of a good father is incalculable, reverberating for generations and shaping the character of his children. I was blessed to have had that kind of dad. He was a wonderful man—not because of his accomplishments or successes. He was great because of the way he lived his life, his devotion to Jesus Christ, and the love he expressed for his family.

My father has been gone since 1977, and I miss him still. I'll never forget the telephone call I received from a minister saying that my dad had suffered a massive heart attack and wasn't expected to live through the night. As I flew to Kansas City, I thought about the memorable times we spent together and the very happiest moments of my childhood.

We would get up very early on a wintry morning, put on our hunting clothes, and head twenty miles out of town to our favorite place. We'd climb over the fence and follow a little creek for several miles leading to an area that I called "the big woods"—because the trees looked so huge to me. Dad would get me situated under a fallen tree that made a secret room, and then we'd wait for the sun to rise. The entire panorama of nature would unfold out there in the woods as the squirrels, chipmunks, and birds awakened before us. Those moments together with my dad were priceless to me. Conversations occurred out there that didn't happen anywhere else. How could I have gotten very angry at a dad who took the time to be with me? The interactions we shared in that setting made me want to be like that man—to adopt his values as my values, his dreams as my dreams, and his God as my God. His pervasive influence continues in my life today.

That's the power of a man to set a kid on the right road. I can think of no wiser investment in the entire realm of human experience.

Home Schooling

W hen our children were young, my wife and I were intent on giving them a good education. In those days we had only two options from which to choose: public schools or private schools. Today, there's a third alternative that warrants consideration.

The fastest-growing educational movement in the world today is the "home-school" phenomenon. More than 1.5 million U.S. parents and millions more in other countries have opted to teach their children at home—not for two or three years, but sometimes as long as twelve.[53] The movement is now old enough to allow for comparisons, and the results have been remarkable.

Universities and colleges are still enrolling their first big wave of home-schooled children, some of whom are the brightest and most well-adjusted students on campus. Standardized tests are verifying the efficiency of home-style learning. Some critics have worried about how home-schooled kids will be properly socialized, but here again the apprehension appears groundless. Almost every city now has a home-school association with activities and athletic leagues, orchestras, and organized field trips to bring the children together.

Admittedly, home schooling is not for everyone, but for those who are willing to pay the price, this third option is an idea whose time has come.

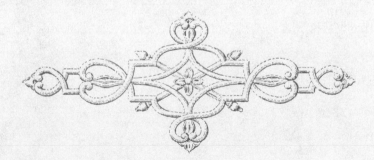

Carving the Stone

Smithsonian magazine once featured a master stonecutter from England named Simon Verity, a man who honed his craft by restoring thirteenth-century cathedrals in Great Britain.

As the authors watched him work, they noticed something very interesting. They wrote, "Verity listens closely to hear the song of the stone under his careful blows. A solid strike, and all is well. A higher-pitched ping, and it could mean trouble. A chunk of rock could break off. He constantly adjusts the angle of the chisel and the force of the mallet to the pitch, pausing frequently to run his hand over the freshly-carved surface."[54]

Verity understood the importance of his task. He knew that one wrong move could be devastating, causing irreparable damage to his work of art. His success was rooted in his ability to read the signals his stones were sending.

In similar fashion, parents need to hone their skills at listening to their children, especially during times of discipline and guidance. It takes a great deal of patience and sensitivity to interpret the child's responses. If you listen carefully, your boys and girls will tell you what they're thinking and feeling.

So whether shaping a child's character or sculpting in stone, the skills needed are crucial to a successful outcome. The honing by the master carver will create a beautiful work of art.

Freedom and Respect

Someone once said, "If you love something, set it free. If it comes back to you, it's yours for life. But if it doesn't come back, it never was yours in the first place." That adage has significant meaning for those who are developing romantic relationships. Let me illustrate.

Some individuals are so needy that they begin to violate the well-known principles of freedom and respect in human interactions. They beg, cry, and grovel for acceptance. Anyone who begins to react that way destroys what is left of the relationship. Just as a drowning person grabs anything that floats, including a rescuer, a panic-stricken lover often tries to hold the one who is attempting to escape. That other person becomes frantic to get away!

I heard about a young man who was determined to win the affection of a girl who refused to even see him. He decided that the way to her heart was through the mail, so he began writing a love letter every day.

When she didn't respond, he increased his output to three notes every twenty-four hours. In all, he wrote more than seven hundred letters in a single summer. Not only did his plan not work—she married the postman! That's the way romantic love works. Appearing too anxious and available actually drives people away rather than attracting them into a committed relationship.

In short, romantic love is one of those rare human endeavors that succeeds best when it requires the least effort. Respect precedes love, and that's why would-be lovers like to nibble at the bait before swallowing the hook.

Men of the Civil War

One of the most fascinating aspects of the U.S. Civil War is the toughness and determination of both Yankee and Rebel soldiers. Their lives were filled with deprivation and danger that is hardly imaginable today. It was common for the troops to march for weeks and then plunge directly into combat without rest. The fighting would continue for days, interspersed with sleepless nights on the ground—sometimes in a freezing rain or snow. The staple was a dry biscuit called hardtack, which shredded their intestinal tracts and left them undernourished.

Men stood rifle to rifle and slaughtered one another like flies. After one particularly bloody battle in 1862, five thousand bodies lay in an area of about two square miles. Many of the wounded remained where they fell for twelve or fourteen hours, with their groans and cries echoing through the countryside.[55]

I'm not glorifying the horrors of war certainly, but I am amazed that the troops didn't crack under these awful circumstances. They were committed to their cause, be they Yankees or Rebels, and nothing was going to deter them.

I do wonder in today's affluent times if our generation would make a similar sacrifice if required to defend our most cherished ideals. Would I? Would you?

The Nurturance of Babies

In the thirteenth century, King Frederick II conducted an experiment with fifty infants to determine what language they would speak if never permitted to hear the spoken word. So he assigned foster mothers to bathe and suckle the children but forbade them to fondle, pet, or talk to their charges. The experiment failed because all fifty infants died. We learned hundreds of years later that babies who aren't touched and cuddled often fail to thrive.

The world has recently been exposed to yet another example of neglected and abused children. Mary Carlson, a researcher from Harvard Medical School, observed an overcrowded Romanian orphanage, where row upon row of babies lay neglected in their cribs. The staff was hopelessly overworked, so the babies were rarely touched even at mealtime. What struck Carlson was the silence in the nursery. There was no crying, no babbling, not even a whimper. Upon physical examinations given at age two, Carlson found that the babies had unusually high amounts of a stress hormone in the blood called cortisol, which is known to damage the brain. Growth was stunted, and the children acted half their age.[56]

It isn't sufficient to feed, clothe, and care for the physical needs of children. It is now clear that touching and nurturance are critical to their survival.

The Antecedents of Disease

W e've been discussing the incredible vulnerability of infants and toddlers. Many investigations in recent years have confirmed that touch and emotional nurturance in the first few years of life are necessary to survival.

Now, a study conducted at Harvard University shows unmistakably that the quality of the bonding between a boy and his mother is related to his physical health forty or fifty years later. Remarkably, 91 percent of college men who said they had not enjoyed a close relationship with their mothers developed coronary artery disease, hypertension, duodenal ulcers, or alcoholism by the midlife years. Only 45 percent of the men who recalled maternal warmth and closeness had similar illnesses. The same was true of men and relationships with their fathers. And consider this: 100 percent of participants in this study whose mothers and fathers were cold and distant suffered numerous diagnosed diseases in midlife.

In short, the quality of early relationships between boys and their parents is a powerful predictor of lifelong health. And you can be sure, the same is true of girls and women.

It comes down to this: When early needs are not met, trouble looms down the road.[57]

Mindy

Mindy was neither a purebred nor a champion, as dogs go. Her daddy had been a travelin' man, so we really didn't know much about her heritage. She was just a scared pup who showed up at the front door late one night after being abused by her owners and then thrown out of a car. We didn't really want another dog, but what could we do?

So we took her in, and she quickly grew to become one of the finest dogs we had ever owned. But Mindy never lost that emotional fragility inflicted by abuse. She couldn't stand to be criticized or scolded when she had accidentally done something wrong. She would actually jump into my lap and hide her eyes.

One summer we went away for a two-week vacation and left Mindy in the backyard. A neighbor boy gave her food and water, but otherwise she was alone most of that time. We obviously underestimated her loneliness or what the isolation would do to her. When we returned, we found her lying next to the house on a blanket surrounded by about seven of our daughter's old stuffed animals. Mindy had found them in a box in the garage and carried them one by one to her bed. She had been desperate for friends!

You know, if an old dog needs love and acceptance in this way, how much more true is it of every child who walks the earth? It's our job as adults to see that each one of them receives the security and love that he or she requires.

The Victimization of Everyone

H as it ever seemed like the whole world is stacked against you—and that you are never given a fair shake? Have you ever said, "Well, what did you expect? Nothing ever goes right for me anyway"?

This defeatist attitude could be expected among those who have been through severe illness, abuse, or disabilities. But something different has been happening in recent years. Large numbers of Americans have begun perceiving themselves as victims of some sort of unfairness—as though someone was out to get them. As more and more individuals perceive themselves in that way, their anger at one another intensifies.

Consider the classifications of some of the people who feel discriminated against. They include Hispanics, African-Americans, Asians, Jews, Native Americans, women, children, the elderly, the sick, the poor, the uneducated, and now even white males, who are not supposed to feel discriminated against. It's what I call the "victimization of everyone."

Now obviously, discrimination, racism, sexism, and ageism are still very serious problems in this culture, and we need to resolve them. I would not underestimate the impact of them. But it doesn't help for people to conclude that they're all being "had" in one way or another. That mind-set is demoralizing. It paralyzes us emotionally, and it leads us to conclude, "What's the use? I can't win!"

Eleanor Roosevelt, who had some very serious handicaps in life, once said, "No one can make you feel inferior without your consent."[58] Well, it's true. And no one can attack your self-worth but you yourself.

Sudden Infant Death Syndrome

You've probably heard about the tragic phenomenon known as sudden infant death syndrome, or SIDS. It's still claiming the lives of about six thousand babies each year in the United States alone.[59]

This killer has mystified medical researchers. Now a study conducted by the U.S. Consumer Product Safety Commission, in collaboration with researchers at the University of Maryland and Washington University-St. Louis, has shed light on the issue. The epidemiologist who directed the investigation, Dr. N. J. Shear, said: "We have not found a cause for SIDS, but our results show that specific items of bedding used in the U.S., such as comforters and pillows, were associated with an increased risk for death to prone sleeping infants whose faces became covered."

This means that babies should not be placed on their stomachs in soft bedding. That precaution will lessen the likelihood that they will rebreathe their own carbon dioxide that's trapped in the blankets and pillows around them. In about 30 percent of the 206 SIDS deaths in the research project, babies were found with bedding pressed against their noses and mouths. The advice now being offered by doctors is that parents place their infants on their backs, not on their stomachs, and that a minimum amount of loose bedding be kept in the crib.[60]

This advice won't eliminate all cases of SIDS, but it could save hundreds, if not thousands, of lives every year.

Home Business

For many families an appealing way to bring extra income into the home is by building a home-based business. Is it possible to work out of your home while still taking care of your children and other duties—and without losing your mind? The answer is yes.

Everything from catering, desktop publishing, pet grooming, sewing, consulting, transcribing legal documents, or even mail-order sales can be done at home. Choosing which business is right for you is the first of three practical steps suggested by Donna Partow, author of a book called *Homemade Business.*[61]

Donna said you can start your own enterprise by taking a personal skills and interest inventory to identify your particular abilities and what you might like doing best. The second step is to do your homework. Begin by asking your librarian to help you research your chosen field. Look up books, magazines, and newspaper articles. Talk to other people who have done what you would most like to do. Join an industry organization and a network. Subscribe to relevant publications, etcetera.

According to Mrs. Partow, the third step is to marshal as much support as you can. Get your children, your spouse, and friends on your side. Setting up a small business can be stressful, and you'll need as much encouragement as you can get.

If you've been torn between family and finances, having a home-based business may turn out to provide for you and your family the best of both worlds.

My Friend Wendy

The year was 1983, and I had an appointment with a young woman who had asked to see me. I was about to meet one of the most unforgettable people I would ever be privileged to know.

Wendy Bergren, the mother of three beautiful little girls, was dying of breast cancer. Doctors had confirmed that the disease was terminal and advised her to go home and prepare to die. But Wendy wouldn't accept their advice. She sought out physicians who would treat her aggressively with chemotherapy, radiation, or anything that might buy a little time. She accepted the certainty of death, but this young mother was determined to live long enough for her newborn baby to remember her. Despite the ordeal that followed, Wendy would not yield to depression and despair. She concentrated, not on herself, but on her children and others in difficult situations. She published a little booklet that listed twenty ways to reach out to families that were struggling from debilitating illnesses. To the end, Wendy was still trying to help those who were hurting.

My young friend died on February 12, 1985. She was courageous to the end. Wendy left behind a loving husband, Scott, and three beautiful, healthy girls. They're almost grown now, and I'm dedicating this commentary to Chrissy, Casey, and Dianna.

How to Help a Sick Mom

In the previous commentary, I wrote about a remarkable young woman named Wendy Bergren, who suffered from terminal breast cancer. In the midst of her terrible ordeal, she penned a little booklet based on her own experience. Her purpose was to offer advice to friends and relatives of mothers with cancer. Wendy listed twenty suggestions to help sick moms and undergird their families when debilitating disease lingers on.

For example, Wendy suggested that friends make it possible for the children of sick mothers to attend birthday parties by bringing some gifts that have already been wrapped for use when needed. And she thought it would be a good idea to make cookie dough and bring it frozen, so sick moms could have the pleasure of baking something fresh for their children.

Wendy also suggested that friends talk about the future. Wendy wrote: "Talk about next week. Next year, ten or twenty years! The power of planning is incredible. Talk to me about my baby's senior graduation, and I can get through next week. Bring travel folders for my silver anniversary trip, or discuss hairstyles for when my hair grows back in. If you look ahead, I can too."

There were seventeen additional suggestions in Wendy's little booklet, but the reader can understand her message. Her purpose was to share her experience with others. This courageous woman brought comfort and kindness to many in the closing days of her life.

Wendy Bergren is gone now, but she will never be forgotten.[62]

The Fine Art of Conversation

Are you tired of those one-word answers your child or teenager gives in response to your questions? You ask how well he played in soccer practice, and he says, "Fine." You wonder how he got along in school today, and he says, "OK." End of the "dialogue."

Well, I have a suggestion that may help. I ran across a simple but very effective way to teach children the art of conversation. It was included in an article written by Sybil Ferguson in *Woman's Day*. I've taught this technique to my own children and hope you will find it helpful too.

Give three tennis balls to your daughter, and ask her to throw them back one at a time. Instead of returning the balls, however, simply hold them. Your daughter will stand there looking at you awkwardly and wondering what to do next. Obviously, it isn't much of a game. Then you explain that good conversation is like that game of catch. One person throws an idea or a comment to the other, and he or she tosses it back. Talking to each other is simply a matter of throwing ideas back and forth.

For example, if you ask your daughter, "How did it go in school today?" and she answers, "Fine," she has caught the ball and held it. We have nothing more to say to each other. But if she responds, "I had a good day because I got an A on my history test," she has caught the ball and thrown it back. I can then ask, "Was it a difficult test?" or "Did you study hard for it?" or "I'll bet you're proud of yourself."[63]

To teach your children how to communicate, simply show them how to catch and throw. Even a very young child can understand that idea. It's just a matter of playing the game.

Predators in the Tall Grass

few years ago my family and I visited the magnificent wild-animal preserve known as the Serengeti in Tanzania. It had rained all day, and we eventually came to a stretch of road that was almost impassable. We were faced with a choice between two muddy paths but had no idea which to take. If we went the wrong way and became stuck, we would have spent the night there without food, water, or bathroom facilities. At that point our seventeen-year-old son, Ryan, volunteered to help.

"I'll run ahead and look at the two roads," he said. "Then I'll wave to let you know which is best."

The missionary who was with us said, "Um, Ryan, I don't think that is a very good idea. You just don't know what might be out there in the tall grass."

Eventually we chose what looked like the better of the two paths. But when we reached the place where the two trails came together, a huge male lion was crouched in the grass off to one side. He rolled his big yellow eyes and dared us to take him on. Ryan looked at that lion and agreed that it might be best to stay in the car!

In a manner of speaking, our experience on the Serengeti illustrates the passage from late adolescence to young adulthood. The journey goes smoothly and safely for some individuals. But a surprisingly large number of teens encounter unexpected "mudholes" that trap and hold them at an immature stage of development. Still others are plagued by dangerous predators. Among these are an addiction to alcohol or drugs, marriage to the wrong person, failure to achieve a coveted dream, suicide, homicide, or other criminal offenses.

It is, alas, *very* easy to make a very big mistake when young. Given the predators lurking in the tall grass, it does behoove us parents to stay very close to our sons and daughters on their road to adulthood.

"But, Daddy . . ."

L et me share an actual letter written by a fourteen-year-old girl about her father, published in *American Girl* magazine. She wrote:

When I was ten, my parents got a divorce. Naturally, my father told me about it, 'cause he was my favorite.

"Honey, I know it's been kind of bad for you these last few days, and I don't want to make it any worse, but there's something I have to tell you. Honey, your mother and I got a divorce."

"But, Daddy . . ."

"Now I know you don't want this, but it has to be done. Your mother and I just don't get along like we used to. I'm already packed, and my plane is leaving in half-an-hour."

"But, Daddy, why do you have to leave?"

Well, honey, your mother and I just can't live together anymore."

"Well I know that, but I mean, why do you have to leave town?"

"Oh, well, I've got someone waiting for me in New Jersey."

"But, Daddy, will I ever see you again?"

"Oh, sure you will, honey. We'll work something out."

"OK, Daddy. Good-bye. Don't forget to write me."

"I won't. 'Bye. Now, go to your room."

"Daddy, I don't want you to go."

"I know, honey, but I have to."

"OK. Well, I guess that's the way life goes sometimes."

After my father walked out that door, I never heard from him again.[64]

The words written by that young girl need no elaboration. But she could tell you so much more!

The Legacy of Divorce

How easily do children cope with the breakup of their family? The findings might surprise you.

California psychologist Judith Wallerstein is one of the most respected authorities on the effects of divorce. She has published numerous books and articles on this subject, including a more recent investigation that should be brought to the attention of every parent. Over the past twenty-five years, Wallerstein tracked hundreds of children of divorce, chronicling their lives from childhood through adolescence—and now through adulthood. Her findings are discouraging.

Wallerstein found that the trauma experienced by young children after a divorce remains with them throughout their lives, making it more difficult to cope with challenges and difficulties. Adolescence and young adulthood are particularly stressful times. Later romantic relationships continue to be influenced by the memories of divorce.

In summary, Wallerstein said, "Unlike the adult experience, the child's suffering does not reach its peak at the breakup and then level off. The effect of the parents' divorce is played and replayed throughout the first three decades of the children's lives."[65]

If you and your spouse are getting a divorce, you should at least consider the consequences of that decision for the most vulnerable members of the family. The research shows that they will never be the same thereafter.

Fetal Alcohol Syndrome

Fetal alcohol syndrome is a condition occurring in babies and children whose mothers indulged in alcoholic beverages during pregnancy. Unfortunately, damage can occur throughout the entire nine months' gestation, but it is especially damaging during the first trimester of development. Alcohol in the blood of the mother at that time can produce devastating problems, including heart anomalies, central nervous system dysfunction, head and facial abnormalities, and lifelong behavior problems. And tragically, fetal alcohol syndrome is thought to be the leading cause of mental retardation.[66]

There is a dramatic reference to alcohol and pregnancy in the Old Testament. You may remember the story of Samson, who terrorized his enemies, the Philistines, with enormous feats of strength. Before Samson was born, his mother was told by an angel that her child was destined for greatness and that she must not weaken him by imbibing strong drink while she was pregnant.[67] As it turns out, the angel knew what he was talking about! Medical science has now verified the wisdom of that advice. That's why a warning to pregnant women is posted, by law, wherever liquor, beer, and wine are sold.

If you're pregnant, or you anticipate becoming pregnant, don't take chances with your baby's future. There is no level of alcohol that is known to be safe. Abstain for the entire nine months. You and your baby will be so glad you did.

Why They Kill

major effort has been made in the past few years to learn why so many teenagers growing up in the inner city are often shockingly violent. What we're seeing now is different from criminal behavior of the past.

Today young people are committing horrible and senseless acts of brutality without remorse—such as the two boys, ages twelve and thirteen, who beat a man to death outside a convenience store just for the pleasure of watching him die. Another boy shot a man sitting in a car at a stop sign. When asked why he did it, the boy said, "Because he looked at me."[68]

After extensive research, scientists have concluded that violent behavior is often related to early child abuse and neglect. When babies spend three days or more in dirty diapers or when they are burned, beaten, or ignored, their blood is flooded with stress hormones—cortisol and adrenaline among others. These hormones bombard and damage the brains of those children. So for the rest of their lives, they will not think and feel what others do. They actually lose the capacity to empathize with those who suffer.[69]

The unmistakable conclusion is that babies and young children are incredibly vulnerable between birth and three years of age. If their families don't protect and care for them, society will pay a terrible price for it in the years to come.

Four on Four

I've always loved the game of basketball, even though I've never been particularly skilled at it. But a few years ago, at age fifty, I had the opportunity of a lifetime. My friends and I had gone to a conference in Laguna, California, which is a beach town populated mostly by surfers and sun worshipers. During an afternoon break, someone suggested that four of us old guys go down to the outdoor basketball court on the beach and challenge the young hotshots who play there. It was a stupid thing to do, but off we went.

When we arrived, about three hundred spectators surrounded the court, where four-man teams waited to take their turn against the reigning champs. We got in the line waiting to play. Rumors began to spread about who these old dudes really were. Some thought we were NBA scouts checking out the talent. Others thought we were coaches from USC or UCLA. Why else would we be there! As for me, I've never been so nervous in my life as I was while waiting to play the champs.

We finally stepped onto the court, and the impossible happened. We got hot and hit everything we shot. Within two minutes, we were ahead by a score of eight to nothing. The crowd went crazy as people began to come from everywhere on the beach. Only three more buckets and we would have pulled off the upset of the century. But then reality set in, and we lost eleven to eight.

Alas, athletic immortality often hangs by the slenderest thread. I missed it by three lousy buckets. How close have you come?

One Horse Open Sleigh

John Pierpont lived and died a failure. At least that's how he might be seen by history. It's not as if he didn't try to find his niche. John poured his heart into everything he did. He just didn't seem to be good at anything.

His career started out with a teaching degree from Yale, but his first position didn't last very long. John was much too easy on his students. So he decided to become a lawyer. He failed at that as well. He opened a dry-goods store but soon went bankrupt. Next, John tried his hand at poetry. He wasn't a bad writer, but he just couldn't earn enough to pay his bills.

John went to school again—this time to become a preacher. His first congregation asked him to resign, so he gave up the ministry. Politics had always intrigued him, so he ran for governor of Massachusetts. He lost big. So he ran for Congress. Again, he lost. Even bigger. Then the Civil War broke out, and he enlisted as a chaplain—but for only two weeks. Eventually, he died at the age of seventy-one while serving as a clerk in the Treasury Department.

John Pierpont's tombstone reads simply: "Poet, preacher, philosopher, philanthropist." Well, one out of four isn't bad. He wrote a simple song somewhere along the way that any three-year-old could sing. The melody and lyrics are as cheerful as Christmas itself. He called it "Jingle Bells," a song about sleighs and horses and snow and laughter.[70]

John Pierpont, though dead and gone, had finally found his niche.

The Longest Task

Have you ever considered how long it takes to raise a human being from birth to maturity and get him or her ready for independent living?

Other creatures do the job much more quickly. Hamsters are ready to go on their own in three weeks. Kittens require only a couple of months; and lion cubs are self-sufficient within two years. Meanwhile, it takes twenty years or more to produce a son or daughter who can earn a living, stay out of trouble, and make normal adult decisions.

Noted author Elisabeth Elliot has written: "There never has been a time when children could successfully be raised without sacrifice and discipline on the part of the parents."[71] There simply aren't any shortcuts or an easy way to do the job right. Let's face it—the child-rearing task is the most protected responsibility we are likely to face. And like any other project worth doing, the important thing is to persevere to the finish line.

Why have I offered this advice today? Because there are many voices out there telling parents to give up, to bail out, to think only of themselves. And there will be many discouraging moments along the way. But as the father of two grown kids, I can tell you that the child-rearing task is worth what it costs us—right through to its conclusion.

The Launch

There is a period in every young adult's life between ages sixteen and twenty-six that can literally shape or break his or her future. I call it the "Critical Decade." A person is transformed during those ten years from a kid who's still living at home and eating at the parents' table to a full-fledged adult, who should be earning a living and taking complete charge of his or her life. Most of the decisions that will shape the next fifty years will be made during this era, including the choice of an occupation, the decision to marry or not to marry, and the establishment of values and principles by which life will be governed.

Some young adults move easily through the critical decade, but others have greater difficulty making decisions and getting on with life. They can't settle on a line of work, set reachable goals, channel their interests, or decide what to do next. So they sit around their parents' home and watch daytime television. Young people such as these remind me of a rocket on a launchpad. They are ready to blast through the stratosphere, but the engines just won't fire. For some, an explosion occurs that leaves debris all over the place.

There are ways to help sons and daughters get moving if they will accept the parents' help. Arrange visits to vocational counselors who can give interest inventories and occupational tests that can clarify goals. Take them on career visits, and introduce them to people working successfully in different professions.

The countdown is coming. Your young adult will either blast off or blow up. You might help make the difference.

Children and Television

There's been considerable debate in recent years about television rating systems. That kind of information is desperately needed by parents who want to protect their kids from harmful content, and I'm among those who believe that the present system just doesn't get the job done.

But even if changes are implemented, there's a new wrinkle to be considered. Social research conducted by Yankelovich Partners, Inc., has recently analyzed the television-viewing habits of Americans. What they discovered is surprising. Forty-two percent of children between nine and seventeen have their own cable or satellite television hookups in their bedrooms.[72] The image of families gathered around a single TV set in the family room is fading. Instead, many kids are off by themselves where they can choose anything that they want to see.

Ann Clurman, a partner at Yankelovich, said, "Almost everything children are seeing is essentially going into their minds in some sort of uncensored or unfiltered way."[73] Considering the explicit sex, violence, nudity, and profanity available now, especially on cable and satellite television, this is a disturbing revelation.

Children need to be protected from adult programming, and yet almost four out of every ten kids have parents who don't really know what they're watching. I fear that situation will come back to haunt us for years to come.

Kids Say the Neatest Things

I love kids, don't you? I like the way they think, the way they talk, and I especially like to read the things that they and their parents write and say.

For example, an eight-year-old girl named Brandy wrote to thank us for a magazine we publish called *Clubhouse*. She said, "Thanks for letting me join in the clud, and thanks to my aunt. You guys are really nicie. I enjoy thoses mageniens. My hoby is cletting rocks, and stunding about the rain fostes. And my favorite subject in school is spelling."

Another little girl came home from the pediatrician and told her daddy that she got shots that day for "mumps, measles, and rebellion." Don't you wish we had an inoculation for that?

And then a mother wrote to say this: "Perhaps there should be a uniform word for 'potty' when children have to go to the bathroom. My three-year-old has been taught to refer to that act as 'a whisper.' Well, his grandfather came to visit us, and in the middle of the night my son came to his bed and said, 'Grandpa, I have to whisper.' Well, not wanting to awaken his wife he said, 'OK. Whisper in my ear.'" And he did.

These delightful moments are what make child rearing so much fun. If your kids have said funny or clever things, I wish you'd send some of those quotes to me.

A Poem

Someone sent me this anonymous little poem the other day that I want to share with you. I don't know who wrote the piece, but I think you're going to like it.

If you can start the day without caffeine; if you can get going without pep pills; if you can always be cheerful, ignoring aches and pains; if you can resist complaining and boring people with your troubles; if you can eat the same food every day and be grateful for it; if you can understand when your loved ones are too busy to give you any time; if you can forgive a friend's lack of consideration; if you can overlook it when those you love take it out on you when, through no fault of your own, something goes wrong; if you can take criticism and blame without resentment; if you can ignore a friend's limited education and never correct him; if you can resist treating a rich friend better than a poor friend; if you can face the world without lies and deceit; if you can conquer tension without medical help; if you can relax without liquor; if you can sleep without the aid of drugs; if you can honestly say that deep in your heart you have no prejudice against creed or color, religion or politics; then, my friend, you're almost as good as your dog. Almost, but not quite.[74]

This poem is dedicated to every dog lover in the world.

Compulsive Parenting

I have expressed concern for years about absentee parents who regularly neglect their children during the developmental years. This problem continues in the fast-paced culture in which we live. But there are other parents—although fewer in number—at the other end of the continuum. It is prevalent among mothers, in particular, who become obsessed by their children. Their responsibilities leave no time for recreational, romantic, or restful activities. And not even the late Mother Teresa would have qualified as a baby-sitter.

Now, I don't question the motives of obsessive parents, but their preoccupation can lead to serious problems. First, making children the centerpiece of life is not in their best interests. It can lead in some cases to overprotection, permissiveness, and dependency.

Second, emotional and physical fatigue produce what is known as *parental burnout.* Just as a battery cannot continually be drained, the human body must be recharged from time to time. Burnout is destructive to the entire family, especially to the children for whom the effort was intended in the first place.

Third, superparenting can also be destructive to a marriage, especially when the mother is the one so inclined. A father may come to resent the children for taking his wife away from him, or she may think her husband is selfish because he won't match her commitment. Either way, a wedge is driven between them that could eventually destroy the family.

It is a pattern that is more common than you might think. Moderation is the key to healthy family life—even in one's approach to parenting.

A Model Soldier

One of my heroes was the great military leader General Douglas MacArthur. He led the Allies to victory over the Japanese during World War II and later commanded the United Nations forces in Korea. MacArthur's surprise landing of his troops at Inchon was one of the most brilliant maneuvers in history. Undoubtedly, he was one of our greatest and most revered military leaders.

I also admire the memory of MacArthur for his respect for families. He was honored in 1942, for example, for being a good father.[75] He was asked to speak on that occasion and made this statement:

> Nothing has touched me more deeply than the act of the National Father's Day committee. By profession, I am a soldier and take great pride in that fact. But I am prouder, infinitely prouder, to be a father. A soldier destroys in order to build. The father only

builds, never destroys. The one has the potentialities of death, the other embodies creation and life. And while the hordes of death are mighty, the battalions of life are mightier still. It is my hope that my son, when I am gone, will remember me not from the battle, but in the home.[76]

Like the old general, I will consider that my earthly existence will have been wasted unless I succeed as a husband and father, and only if God is ultimately pleased with me. There is no higher calling to which I could aspire.

Fame

Society's fascination with Hollywood and celebrities has gone a little crazy. Millions idolize those who have achieved fame and fortune, but stardom does not provide the satisfaction that it advertises. Marilyn Monroe could have told us that.

Consider the adoration and respect accorded to Muhammad Ali in his prime. He was known around the world as "the prize fighter who couldn't be beaten." His picture appeared on the cover of *Sports Illustrated* more times than any athlete in history. Wherever he went, the cameras followed. Today, though, it's a different story.

Sportswriter Gary Smith spent some time with the ailing fighter at his home and asked to see his trophy room. Ali escorted him to a dark, damp barn beside his house. There, leaning against one wall was a board displaying mementos, photos from the "Thrilla in Manila," pictures of Ali dancing and punching and hoisting championship belts over his head. But the pictures were smeared with white streaks. Pigeons had made their home in the rafters. Ali picked up the board and turned it around, face to the wall. Then, as he started to leave, Smith heard him mumble, "I had the world, and it wasn't nothin'. Look now."[77]

Fame is fleeting, even for those few who achieve it. If that is where you are searching for meaning, you are not likely to find it.

"The Game of Life"

When my daughter, Danae, was a teenager, she came home one day and said, "Hey, Dad! There's a great new game out. I think you'll like it. It's called Monopoly." I just smiled.

We gathered the family together and set up the board. It didn't take the kids long to figure out that old Dad had played this game before. I soon owned all the best properties, including Boardwalk and Park Place. I even had Baltic and Mediterranean. My kids were squirming, and I was loving every minute of it.

About midnight I foreclosed on the last property and did a little victory dance. My family wasn't impressed. They went to bed and made me put the game away. As I began putting all of my money back in the box, a very empty feeling came over me. Everything that I had accumulated was gone. The excitement over riches was just an illusion. And then it occurred to me, *Hey, this isn't just the game of Monopoly that has caught my attention; this is the game of life. You sweat and strain to get ahead, but then one day, after a little chest pain or a wrong change of lanes on the freeway, the game ends. It all goes back in the box.* You leave this world just as naked as the day you came into it.

I once saw a bumper sticker that proclaimed, He who dies with the most toys wins. That's wrong. It should say, He who dies with the most toys dies anyway.

Of Elephants and Teenagers

O ther than dogs, which I have always loved, the animals that fascinate me most are elephants. These magnificent creatures are highly intelligent and have very complex emotional natures. I suppose that's what makes it disturbing when we see them suffering the encroachment of civilization.

That is happening in the Pilanesberg National Park in Northwestern South Africa. Rangers there have reported that young bull elephants in that region have become increasingly violent in recent years—especially to nearby white rhinos. Without provocation, they knock them over and then kneel and gore them to death. This is not typical elephant behavior, and it has been very difficult to explain.

But now game wardens think they've cracked the code. Apparently, the aggressiveness is a by-product of government programs to reduce elephant populations by killing the older animals. Almost all of the young rogues were orphaned when they were calves, depriving them of adult contact. Under normal circumstances, dominant older males keep the young bulls in line and serve as role models for them. In the absence of that influence, juvenile delinquents grow up to terrorize their neighbors.[78]

Now, I know it's risky to apply animal behavior too liberally to human begins, but the parallel here is too striking to miss. Thirty percent of all American children were born out of wedlock, and in the African-American community, the number is above 70 percent.[79] Most of these kids grow up without masculine role models and discipline. The result is often catastrophic—for teenagers *and* for elephants.

Endnotes

1. Max Lucado, *In the Eye of the Storm: A Day in the Life of Jesus* (Dallas: Word, 1991), 11.

2. David Elkind, *The Hurried Child* (Reading, Mass.: Addison-Wesley, 1981).

3. L. M. Boyd, *Boyd's Book of Odd Facts* (New York: Signet, 1980), 50.

4. James C. Dobson, *Straight Talk* (Dallas: Word, 1991), 33–34.

5. William Manchester, *The Death of a President* (New York: HarperCollins, 1988).

6. Erma Bombeck, "Fragile Strings Join Parent, Child," *Arizona Republic,* 15 May 1977.

7. Anonymous.

8. Desmond Morris, *Intimate Behavior*, rev. ed. (New York: Kodansha America, 1997), 72–103.

9. Anne Stewart, "The American Way," *Associated Press, 23 November 1997.* http://www.ap.org/

10. National Debt Clock, maintained by the Concord Coalition.

11. Denise Duclax, "Questions about the 'Inheritance Boom,'" *American Bankers Association Journal* (December 1996): 47.

12. John Sedgwick, *Rich Kids: America's Young Heirs and Heiresses, How They Love and Hate Their Money* (New York: William Morrow and Company, 1985).

13. Greg Harrington, "Ears to You: Protecting Your Hearing Now to Help Avoid Problems When You're Older," *Atlanta Journal and Constitution,* 19 January 1998.

14. Dick Korthals, "A Gentle Touch," Focus on the Family, 1992.

15. General Douglas MacArthur, *Duty, Honor, Country,* given at West Point, 12 May 1962.

16. Bonnie Miller Rubin, "Taking Showers at School Is Going Down the Drain," *Chicago Tribune,* 26 March 1996.

17. Dennis Overbye, "The Wizard of Space and Time," *Omni* (February 1979): 46.

18. Charles Swindoll, *Come Before Winter* (Sisters, Oreg.: Multnomah, 1985), 36.

19. L. M. Boyd, *Boyd's Book of Odd Facts* (New York: Signet, 1980), 93.

20. David Swoap, president of Hope International, telephone conversation with Craig Osten, assistant to author, 1995.

21. Peter Blackburn, "Homeless Children Killed in Brazil," *Reuters,* 3 March 1992. http://www.reuters.org/

22. P. W. Juscyzk and E. A. Hohne, "Infants' Memory for Spoken Words," *Science,* (26 September 1997): 1984 ff.

23. Rachel Ellis, "Parents Beware: Little Ears Are Listening," *Associated Press,* 26 September 1997. http://www.ap.org/

24. *Final Report of the Attorney General's Commission on Pornography* (Nashville: Rutledge Hill Press, 1987).

25. Harriet Chiang and Ramon G. McLeod, "Net Porn Law Shot Down," *San Francisco Chronicle,* 27 June 1997.

26. "White House Attorney Found Dead," *Associated Press,* 20 July 1993. http://www.ap.org/

27. "Reflections by Vincent Foster on Law and His Life," *National Law Journal* (23 August 1993): 31.

28. James C. Dobson, *The New Dare to Discipline* (Wheaton, Ill.: Tyndale House Publishers, 1992), 105–106.

29. John Donne, "Devotions Upon Emergent Occasions," in John Bartlett, *Familiar Quotations*, ed. Justin Kaplan, 16th ed. (Boston: Little, Brown and Company, 1992), 231.

30. Thomas J. Bouchard, et al., "Sources of Human Psychological Differences: The Minnesota Study of Twins Reared Apart," *Science* (12 October 1990): 223.

31. "Twins Separated at Birth: The Story of Jim Lewis and Jim Springer," *Smithsonian* (October 1980).
    http://www.modcult.brown.edu/students/angell/Jimtwins.html

32. Oliver Wendell Holmes, "The Last Leaf on the Tree," 1895.
    http://www.cs.cmu.edu/People/johnmil/poems/LastLeaf.html

33. Karl Murray, "The 36th (Ulster) Division, and the Battle of the Somme, 1916," *The Great War: 1914-1918* (1996).
    http://www.infosites.net/general/the-great-war/

34. Ibid.

35. *East Gate Newsletter,* April 1997.

36. *World Book Encyclopedia,* 1996, s.v. "Taj Mahal."

37. Quoted by Max Lucado, *The Applause of Heaven* (Dallas: Word, 1990), 132.

38. Ibid.

39. David Herbert Donald, *Lincoln* (New York: Touchstone Books, 1995).

40. Charles Neidler, *The Autobiography of Mark Twain* (New York: HarperPerrenial, 1990).

41. "Courage Performed Outside the Olympics by Its Athletes," *CBS Evening News,* 8 February 1998.

42. Isaiah 53:6, NIV.

43. Study done by Penn State University and reported in *Archives of Pediatric and Adolescent Medicine* (December 1997).

44. "U.S. Naval Institute Proceedings," as quoted by Stephen Covey, *The Seven Habits of Highly Effective People* (New York: Simon & Schuster, 1989), 33.

45. *Family News in Focus,* 6 March 1992.

46. "Needle Park Closes," *CNN,* 26 February 1992.

47. Stella Chess M.D., and Alexander Thomas, M.D., *Know Your Child: An Authoritarian Guide for Today's Parents* (New York: Basic Books, 1987), 33.

48. Peter Brimelow, "The Lost Children," *Forbes* (29 December 1997).

49. *Fatal Addiction,* Focus on the Family Films, 1989.

50. Marilyn Elias, "Family Dinners Nourish Ties with Teenagers," *USA Today,* 18 August 1997.

51. "A Community in Crisis," *Focus on the Family* daily broadcast, 5 January 1998.

52. Linda Roach Monroe, "An Exercise in Common Sense: You Don't Have to Knock Yourself Out at the Gym to Live Longer," *Los Angeles Times,* 20 February 1990.

53. Home School Legal Defense Association, http://*www.hslda.org*

54. Per Ola D'Aulaire and Emily D'Aulaire, "Now What Are They Doing at That Crazy St. John the Divine?" *Smithsonian* (December 1992): 32.

55. National Park Service, "Battle at Antietam, September 17, 1862," *Civil War Summaries by Campaign.* http://www2.cr.nps.gov/abpp/battles/md003.htm

56. Janet McConnaughey, "Study of Romanian Orphans Shows Importance of Touch," *Associated Press,* 28 October 1997. http://www.ap.org/

57. "Parent's Love Affects Child's Health" *Reuters,* 10 March 1997. http://www.reuters.org/

58. John Bartlett, *Familiar Quotations* ed. Justin Kaplan, 16th ed. (Boston: Little, Brown and Company, 1992), 654.

59. Eric Schoch, "Doctors Offer Tips on Avoiding Infant Deaths," *Indianapolis Star,* 16 June 1995.

60. N. J. Shears, M.D., *Infant Suffocation Project—Final Report,* U.S. Consumer Product Safety Commission, January 1995.

61. Donna Partow, *Homemade Business* (Colorado Springs, Colo.: Focus on the Family Publishing, 1991).

62. *Mom Is Very Sick: Here's How to Help,* Focus on the Family. Out of print.

63. Sybil Ferguson, *Woman's Day* (17 February 1980).

64. Vicki Kraushaar, "That's the Way Life Goes Sometimes," (July 1976). Reprinted by permission from *American Girl,* a magazine for all girls published by Girl Scouts of the U.S.A.

65. Barbara Vobejda, "Children of Divorce Heal Slowly, Study Finds; Scholar's Latest Evidence in Influential Series," *Washington Post,* 3 June 1997.

66. *Fetal Alcohol Syndrome Factsheet,* Missouri Department of Mental Health, Division of Alcohol and Drug Abuse.

67. Judges 13.

68. "The Family at the End of the 20th Century," *Focus on the Family* daily broadcast, 8–9 June 1995.

69. Ronald Kotulak, "Children's Brains May Change in Response to Stress," *Washington Post,* 31 August 1993.

70. Robert Fulghum, *It Was on Fire When I Lay Down on It,* (New York: Villard Books, 1989), 17–20.

71. Elisabeth Elliot, *Discipline: The Glad Surrender* (Ada, Mich.: Fleming H. Revell, 1985),

72. "Yankelovich Monitor," Yankelovich Partners, Norwalk, Connecticut. http://www.yankelovich.com

73. Ibid.

74. Sam Venable, "Live a Dog's Life? We Lowly Humans Aren't That Lucky," *Knoxville News-Sentinel,* 24 March 1998.

75. Jane Fullerton, "LR Doctor Joins Team for Reform," *Arkansas Democrat-Gazette,* 28 May 1994.

76. Dale Turner, "'Dagwood' Image Hides the True Value of Fatherhood—It's No Minor Task to Mold Young Lives," *Seattle Times,* 19 June 1993.

77. Gary Smith, "Ali and His Entourage," *Sports Illustrated* (16 April 1988): 48–49.

78. Michael D. Lemonick, "Young, Single and Out of Control," *Time* (13 October 1997).

79. "Births to Teens, Unmarried Women, and Prenatal Care 1985–1994," *Statistical Abstract of the United States, 1997,* table no. 96, p. 78.

Index